Social Problems

This short book lays out a new definition for what constitutes a social problem: the violation of a group's human rights, which are understood as commonly upheld standards about what people deserve and should be protected from in life. Evaluating U.S. society from an international human rights perspective, Bonds also stresses that human rights are necessarily political and can therefore never be part of a purely objective exercise to assess wellbeing in a particular society. His approach recognizes that there is no one single interpretation of what rights mean, and that different groups with differing interests are going to promote divergent views, some better than others. This book is ideal for undergraduate sociology courses on social problems, as well as courses on social justice and human rights.

Eric Bonds is an assistant professor of sociology at the University of Mary Washington. Dr. Bonds' research has appeared in several scholarly publications, including the *Journal of World-Systems Research*, *Critical Sociology*, *Societies Without Borders*, and *Peace Review*. He teaches courses in environmental sociology and social issues.

Framing 21st Century Social Issues

Series Editor: France Winddance Twine, University of California–Santa Barbara

The goal of this new, unique series is to offer readable, teachable "thinking frames" on today's social problems and social issues by leading scholars. These are available for view on http://routledge.custom-gateway.com/routledge-social-issues.html

For instructors teaching a wide range of courses in the social sciences, the Routledge *Social Issues Collection* now offers the best of both worlds: originally written short texts that provide "overviews" to important social issues *as well as* teachable excerpts from larger works previously published by Routledge and other presses.

As an instructor, click to the website to view the library and decide how to build your custom anthology and which thinking frames to assign. Students can choose to receive the assigned materials in print and/or electronic formats at an affordable price.

Available

The Enduring Color Line in U.S. Athletics
Krystal Beamon and Chris M. Messer

Identity Problems in the Facebook Era
Daniel Trottier

The Pains of Mass Imprisonment
Benjamin Fleury-Steiner and Jamie G. Longazel

From Trafficking to Terror
Constructing a Global Social Problem
Pardis Mahdavi

Unequal Prospects
Is Working Longer the Answer?
Tay McNamara and John Williamson

Beyond the Prison Industrial Complex
Crime and Incarceration in the 21st Century
Kevin Wehr and Elyshia Aseltine

Girls with Guns
Firearms, Feminism, and Militarism
France Winddance Twine

Terror
Social, Political, and Economic Perspectives
Mark Worrell

Torture
A Sociology of Violence and Human Rights
Lisa Hajjar

DIY
The Search for Control and Self-Reliance in the 21st Century
Kevin Wehr

Foreign Remedies
What the Experience of Other Nations Can Tell Us about Next Steps in Reforming U.S. Health Care
David A. Rochefort and Kevin P. Donnelly

Social Problems
A Human Rights Perspective

Eric Bonds
University of Mary Washington, Fredericksburg

Routledge
Taylor & Francis Group

NEW YORK AND LONDON

First published 2015
by Routledge
711 Third Avenue, New York, NY 10017

and by Routledge
2 Park Square, Milton Park, Abingdon, Oxon, OX14 4RN

Routledge is an imprint of the Taylor & Francis Group, an informa business

Library of Congress Cataloging-in-Publication Data
Bonds, Eric, 1976-Social problems : a human rights perspective / Eric Bonds.
pages cm. – (Framing 21st century social issues)
1. Human rights–United States. 2. Social problems–United States.
3. Social justice–United States. 4. Human rights. 5. Social problems. 6. Social justice. I. Title.
JC599.U5B584 2014
323.0973–dc23
2013050741

ISBN: 978-0-415-73712-8 (pbk)
ISBN: 978-1-317-81618-8 (ebk)

Typeset in Adobe Garamond Pro
by Cenveo Publisher Services

I dedicate this book to my students, past, present, and future. With love and hope.

Contents

Series Foreword

The early years of the 21st century have been a time of paradoxes. Growing prosperity and the growth of the middle classes in Brazil, China, India, and South Africa have been accompanied by climate change, growing inequality, environmental degradation, labor exploitation, gendered violence, state censorship of social media, governmental corruption, and human rights abuses. Sociologists offer theories, concepts and analytical frames that enable us to better understand the challenges and cultural transformations of this century. One goal of this series is inspired by the following question: "How can we generate new forms of collective knowledge that can help solve some of our local, global, and transnational problems?"

We live in a world in which new communication technologies and products such as cell phones, iPads, and new social media such as Facebook, Google, Skype and Twitter have transformed online education, global communication networks, local and transnational economies, and facilitated revolutions such as the "Arab Spring." These same technologies have generated new forms of entertainment, employment, protest, and pleasure. Social media have been utilized by social justice activists, political dissidents, educators, entrepreneurs, and multinational corporations. They have also been a source of corporate criminality and government corruption—used as forms of surveillance that threaten democracy, privacy, creative expression, and political freedoms.

The goal of this series is provide accessible and innovative analytical frames that examine a wide range of social issues, including social media, whose impact is local, global, and transnational. Sociologists are ideally poised to contribute to a global conversation about a range of issues such as the impact of mass incarceration on intimacy, family formation, local economies, medical technologies, health disparities, violence, torture, transnational migration, militarism, and the AIDS epidemic.

This is the fifth year of the Routledge Social Issues Book Series. The books in this series introduce analytical frames that dissect and discuss social problems and social pleasures. These books also engage and intervene directly in current debates within the social sciences over how best to define, rethink, and respond to the social issues that characterize the early 21st century. The contributors to this series bring together theories from classical sociology into dialogue with contemporary social theorists from interdisciplinary and diverse intellectual traditions, including but not limited to feminist, Marxist, and European social theory.

Readers do not need an extensive background in academic sociology to benefit from these books. The books explore contemporary social problems in ways that introduce basic sociological concepts in the social sciences, cover key literature in the field, and offer original diagnoses. Our series includes books on a wide range of topics including climate change, consumption, eugenics, torture, surrogacy, gun violence, social media, sports, and youth culture. Each book is student-friendly in that we provide glossaries of terms for the uninitiated that appear in bold in the text. Each chapter ends with questions for further thought and discussion. The books are the ideal level for undergraduates because they are accessible without sacrificing a theoretically sophisticated and innovative analysis.

Eric Bonds asks us to rethink and reframe the issue of human rights from a focus on the international arena to an analysis of the United States. Bonds provides an expansive notion of human rights by considering the normative expectations of a dignified and meaningful life in the United States. This book brings together a number of issues that can be considered in human rights evaluation, including poverty, sexual violence, a living wage, policing, and racial inequalities. By shifting the focus to intersecting forms of inequality and inhumanity in the United States, Bonds reframes analyses of "human rights" by focusing on the United States and the conditions of the impoverished, incarcerated, unemployed or underemployed, and asking the reader to consider what changes in our public policies would move us towards a more humane system in the United States. This book is ideal for courses on public policy, social inequality, social justice, social problems, and human rights.

France Winddance Twine
University of California–Santa Barbara

Preface

The study of social problems is a longstanding, sizable, and lively sub-discipline within sociology. Students might find it funny to learn, however, that there is no agreement about what actually constitutes a "social problem" or not. Perhaps this is one of the reasons why the study of social problems has been so successful as an academic enterprise; "social problems" can mean so many things to so many different people that anyone within the subfield can study or teach almost anything he or she wants. But this lack of a common agreement is debilitating as well. Injustices and suffering are real, but we sociologists often lack a common framework to distinguish these as legitimate social problems as opposed to the so called "epidemics," crazes, and supposed "crime waves" that we are often told plague our society, but upon further inspection are not really so widespread or troublesome at all.

My primary goal in this book is to provide a new definition for what constitutes a social problem. I define it as *the violation of a group's human rights*, which I describe as commonly upheld standards about what people deserve and should be protected from in life that have been codified by some widely recognized international body. I use the **Universal Declaration of Human Rights**, which is included in the Appendix of this book, as a paradigmatic expression of shared standards about the treatment of persons in the contemporary world. I will argue that the Universal Declaration of Human Rights can be used as a tool to evaluate U.S. society.

However, I also recognize that human rights are defined and understood within the context of intersecting forms of social inequality and struggles for political power. Using human rights to evaluate wellbeing can therefore never be part of a purely objective academic exercise. The approach that I advocate recognizes that there is no one single interpretation of what rights mean, and that different groups with differing interests are going to promote divergent views. Even so, I argue that some interpretations are better than others. Interpretations that recognize the worth of all persons, that seek to maximize wellbeing across society, and—where appropriate—that strike a balance between groups with conflicting interests are, in my view, the most useful.

The achievement of rights, as lived realities rather than idealized standards, involves building the grassroots movements necessary to change government policies. To this end, I offer several public policy alternatives intended to inspire student discussions and to help students consider ways that we in the United States can move towards fulfilling this objective. I describe various strategies U.S. social movements have used in the recent past to win important human rights victories. I hope that the perspective I provide in this book will give students the conceptual tools to look at U.S. society in new ways, and that some of the ideas expressed here will be useful in their lives that lie ahead.

Acknowledgments

I would like to extend my thanks to France Winddance Twine for supporting this project, and also for all the excellent edits and advice she provided. She taught me a great deal. I would also like to thank Leslie Martin and Kristina Kahl for the ideas, feedback, and inspiration they gave me as I was writing this book, but also, for longer still, as I've been teaching a class in "social problems." Mostly, I would like to acknowledge the support I receive from Emily Taylor, to whom I am grateful for helping make this book possible, but also for so much more.

1: Introduction to the Human Rights Perspective

We live in a turbulent, dramatic time. In many parts of the globe, the world is quite literally being remade before our very eyes. Human rights is one of the forces motivating these changes. For instance, when we learn that while indigenous people in Bolivia (who make up a majority of that nation's 10 million people) have for centuries lived as second-class citizens in their own land, but have recently ushered into office an indigenous president who has transformed the nation's government, we can interpret this as, in part, an issue of human rights. Likewise, the story of Mohamed Bouazizi, a twenty-six-year-old fruit vendor in Tunisia, also has something to do with human rights. When he set himself on fire in protest at the routine abuse he suffered at the hands of corrupt officials looking for bribes on December 17, 2010, he sparked an uprising in his own country, which then spread throughout North Africa and the Middle East in what has come to be known as the Arab Spring. This wave of unrest was then followed by the Occupy Movement in North America and Europe. This unexpected and remarkable series of events demonstrated again that human rights were an issue of international significance.

But human rights stories do not simply happen elsewhere. Eleanor Roosevelt, the former First Lady and wife of Franklin Delano Roosevelt (1933–1945) and one of the drafters of the Universal Declaration of Human Rights, once asked, "Where do human rights begin?" The answer, she said, is "in small places, close to home—so close and so small that they cannot be seen on any maps of the world. Yet they are the world of the individual person." Human rights begin when people across the world, including those living in the United States, expect to live with justice and dignity, and to have the opportunity to develop and grow as individuals.

Human rights are one way to measure progress in human societies. They are a way of knowing when things are going as we might hope. When, for instance, an unemployed parent receives temporary government support in the form of checks that can help pay the mortgage on her family's house until she is able to find another job, this can be considered a issue of human rights. When a low-income parent who is underpaid receives nutritional assistance in the form of food stamps to help feed his children, this can also be defined as a human rights issue. And it also has something to do with human rights when a graduating high school senior who shows great academic promise, but whose family does not have the financial resources to pay for college, receives a grant from the federal government to help pay her way.

As the above examples indicate, we can use a human rights framework to assess our society in terms of our shared values, but this applies not only when things are going well, but also when our society fails to live up to our collective expectations. When justice is lacking, dignity is denied, and when the futures of young people are being deflated by the absence of socially meaningful employment and huge student loan debts, rather than being filled with all the opportunities and hope young people deserve, then concerns about human rights should be brought to the fore. In this book I will employ the notion of human rights as a way to indicate that there is a "**social problem**," for instance when children grow up in poverty, when police use racial profiling, or when some racial groups are profoundly overrepresented in our nation's jails. By defining a social problem as the denial of the human rights of a group, this approach clarifies (in an era in which we are constantly being bombarded with "problems") whether a social problem is real, and is not simply some aspect of the world that has been sensationalized to catch our attention.

The Social Construction of Social Problems

It is important to note that some things that are often defined as "problems" may not really be so troublesome after close inspection. For instance, not too long ago my inbox was filled up over a period of a couple of weeks by several professors at the university where I teach. These professors were sending numerous emails out to the faculty email list complaining to one another about what they collectively saw as the dismal academic performance of their students, compared to cohorts in years passed. These professors were bemoaning that students, according to what they believed, were less well prepared for college than those from earlier generations, having lower reading, writing, and math skills. Now, we could take these complaints on face value and change our class structures and provide more remedial services at our colleges and universities, or we could put these claims within their historical context and think about them critically.

This is what sociologist Joel Best (2011) advocates, when he argues that "stupidity epidemics" are recurring crises that happen in American society. The thing is, according to Best, there is actually no evidence that recent generations have been less well educated by our public schools. Rather, schools are constantly being reformed in American society. And reformers who would like to implement new educational policies may seek to grab our attention by telling us what dire straits our schools are in (as they hope, of course, to convince us of the need for their new program). This **claims-making** influences how Americans in general think about education and the intelligence of young people.

So going back to that flurry of email complaints from professors at my university, there probably is not much reason to believe that students are any less well prepared for college than other generations, even if the situation has been widely defined as such. But this defining process is critical, to Best (2011) and to other sociologists, because definitions of the world can have real consequences. In this case, maybe it resulted in professors changing their classes to make them less challenging, or maybe professors altered their grading practices by scoring tests and assignments either more strictly or in a more relaxed manner compared to the time when they were sure that students were, supposedly, better prepared for college work.

Beyond the "stupidity epidemic," Best gives us another great example of a "non-problem" social problem in his study of Halloween candy sabotage (Best and Horiuchi 1985). We've all heard about the dangers some strangers may pose when they place razor blades or poison in the candy that they randomly give out to the children who are trick-or-treating in the neighborhood. Best points out, however, that there are no actual instances when this happened, at least in regard to the children of strangers. But the perceptions, even though based on false or exaggerated claims, have real consequences. When I was growing up, Halloween was a kind of neighborhood candy free-for-all. But for my children it's a much more closely monitored affair, and probably something a little less fun.

The examples of Halloween and "stupidity epidemics" help us understand the social construction of social problems. **Social constructionism** draws from a long intellectual tradition that asserts that people do not act based upon the world itself, but rather based upon interpretations or definitions of that world. Early American sociologist W. I. Thomas perhaps summed up the social constructionist position best when he said, "if men (or people) define situations as real, they are real in their consequences" (quoted in Merton 1995). To social constructionists studying social problems, nothing in the world is inherently problematic. Some things simply get defined that way (Spector and Kitsuse 1977). Social constructionists argue that a tremendous amount of evidence can be used to bolster this point, because what is defined as a problem in one particular society at one particular point in time may not be defined as such in others. These definitions, though, become consequential because they provide motivations for human action. In the case of Halloween, our collective definition of the situation makes us more reluctant to send our children out to gather candy from neighbors, and in the case of "stupidity epidemics," we perpetually change our educational policies and practices to—hopefully—produce smarter kids.

A social constructionist perspective is invaluable to the study of many phenomena defined as social problems because it gives us some intellectual tools that can help us think critically. We are perpetually being told to be concerned about "social problems" out there in the world. For instance, we might hear about the supposed problem of "internet addiction," which is allegedly altering the brains of young people and making them mentally dependent upon their digital worlds, something akin to, and potentially just as debilitating as, alcoholism or drug addiction (Fox News 2012). Or we might hear about "sex addiction epidemics" in which a supposedly increasing number of people, fueled by the availability of online porn, are risking their physical and emotional wellbeing by seeking frequent sexual encounters (Lee 2011). Such news reporting of "social problems" has much to do with the social organization of major media outlets in America. Today in the United States, most news media organizations are businesses that ensure their profitability by doing two main things: pushing costs down and attracting viewers' attention to keep advertising revenue up. By giving us sensational stories about "epidemics" and by warning us about new "addictions" sweeping across the nation, news organizations can accomplish both goals: they give us an entertaining story that costs practically nothing to produce.

Rather than jumping on the bandwagon and declaring these things to be "real" problems, the perspective of social constructionism allows us to study the **careers of social problems** as claims-making processes, which begin when writers, experts, or activists first define something as problematic (Best 2013; Spector and Kitsuse 1977). News organizations may pick up these claims, but with little money to pay investigative reporters to subject them to any real scrutiny. On the contrary, reporters might instead sensationalize the stories—overgeneralizing from a few isolated incidents and exaggerating consequences—in order to attract readers and viewers. These claims might then be picked up by members of the public as appropriate definitions of reality, and politicians looking to score points with constituents may act to craft policies in order to address such so called "problems" (see Best 2013 for one elaboration of this process). While coverage of such social "problems" likely does little to advance the public interest, it does make sense when we understand news organizations as businesses that are working to keep and attract audiences with limited budgets for in-depth reporting. Such "problems," of course, may not really be so bad after all when subjected to some scrutiny and critical thinking. But to social constructionists, this is hardly the point. After all, when certain aspects of the world become defined as problems, people change their behavior accordingly, sometimes in very significant ways.

The Human Rights Approach

Social constructionism holds powerful analytic insights and can teach some important lessons about the world in which we live, but it is not in itself sufficient for a fully developed study of social problems. Social constructionism emphasizes the relativity of social problems. What is taken as a problem in one historic time and place may not be treated as such in another. After all, we can look to see that while child abuse and neglect are treated as grievous social problems today, this was not always the case. In American society, these concepts have a relatively recent history; 100 years ago such behavior was not deemed illegal. We might also consider the practice of slavery, which today we hold as an abomination, but was once a common and, at least for some, a taken-for-granted feature of American society.

But are we really comfortable with this position of **moral relativism**, which holds that no condition is inherently problematic? One difficulty with this position is that while we might observe that society-at-large may not seem to interpret certain conditions as problematic, for instance slavery or child abuse in 19th-century America, this does not mean they were not experienced as deeply troubling by the individuals who lived under these conditions. In other words, it's not that these conditions weren't problematic for slaves or for children living in abusive homes, it's just that for the most part these individuals lacked the social power necessary to express their suffering in terms that would be recognized and deemed legitimate by the rest of America. So how can we reconcile the academic perspective of social constructionism—which holds that nothing is inherently problematic—along with an acknowledgment that human suffering is real, and has an objective reality? Social theorist Bryan Turner (2006) argues that this might be done through human rights.

At least three conditions may be deemed objectively problematic because, whenever they are experienced, they cause suffering: pain, indignity, and insecurity. Although pain and suffering is a universal experience that practically all people who live long enough feel, this does not mean it is universally tolerated (Turner 2006). Rather, we work to protect ourselves and others (but typically not animals) from pain, and once experienced, we seek its amelioration. **Indignity**, we might say, is social pain, experienced when one is unable to fulfill the conditions that constitute normal personhood within any given society. **Insecurity**, on the other hand, occurs when one's existence, or the continued existence of one's family, is threatened. This may mean living at serious risk of physical attack, but also might mean living day to day without knowing where one will find the next meal, or how one will house and clothe one's children.

Suffering, in other words, is real. Human rights, according to Turner (2006), are the means by which contemporary societies acknowledge our shared vulnerability to pain and suffering and act to ameliorate it. Other theorists have sought to justify human rights not just based on our shared capacity to suffer, as Turner (2006) does, but also on a shared recognition that all persons have the potential to contribute to the development of the societies in which they are born (Sen 1999). Some sociologists think of human rights in a different way, as claims upon social power arrangements that are required to promote human life and dignity in the aftermath of the cataclysmic wars in the early half of the twentieth century (Sjoberg, Gill, and Williams 2001). Regardless of how sociologists theorize the basis of human rights, all agree that they are not "natural." They are not "inalienable," nor are they timeless. Rather human rights, from a sociological perspective, must be viewed as common agreements about the treatment of persons within particular historic contexts.

Human rights, then, are social constructions, which we will simply define as broadly shared agreements, codified through some widely recognized deliberative body, about what every person deserves and should be protected from in life simply on account of being born into our contemporary global society. While human rights are social constructions, there is also something special about them. They are widely agreed upon norms and ethical guidelines with centuries-long histories of conflict and consensus, forged through grassroots advocacy, the development of governments, and globalization (see Blau and Moncado 2009; Tilly 1990; Wallerstein 2011). While there is no one definitive list of human rights, a very good place to start is with the Universal Declaration.

When the Universal Declaration of Human Rights was being drafted between 1947 and 1948, it's no exaggeration to say that the world had just been shattered by events in the preceding 40 years. Both World War I and World War II rank among the deadliest sprees of violence in human history, the first war claiming 37 million lives. The Second World War killed over 60 million persons, devastating practically all of Europe, Japan, and significant areas elsewhere in Asia and North Africa. The moral consciousness of the world was roused not only by the scale of these catastrophes, but also by the particular horror of the Nazi genocide, involving the systematic murder of 6 million Jews along with millions of individuals, part of the Roma ethnic group, prisoners of war, and homosexuals. In between these two terrible periods of violence was a global economic depression in the 1930s. The global economic slowdown was so severe—driving unemployment up to 25 percent in the United States, for instance—that many levelheaded people wondered if capitalism, as a form of social organization, would survive.

In this international context, the newly formed United Nations responded to pressure from **civil society** groups and national governments by establishing a committee to write an "international bill of rights" (Morsink 1999). The Declaration is an international document, having been drafted by representatives from eight different nations, and having been adopted by the United Nations with 48 votes. Importantly, while eight countries abstained from voting either up or down, no nation in the world cast a vote against the adoption of the Universal Declaration[1] (Morsink 1999). The document states, in its preamble, that

> Disregard and contempt for human rights have resulted in barbarous acts which have outraged the conscience of mankind, and the advent of a world in which human beings shall enjoy freedom of speech and belief and freedom from fear and want has been proclaimed as the highest aspiration of the common people.

All this is to say that the drafters of this document—living in the wake of a terrible global economic depression, two devastating world wars, and the Nazi Holocaust—hoped to establish an international framework that could help secure a more hopeful future.

The Universal Declaration of Human Rights has been immensely significant in our particular era. While it is not, of course, a legally binding treaty, it did provide the framework for subsequent international agreements, like the International Covenant on Political and Civil Rights, the International Covenant on Economic, Social, and Cultural Rights, and the International Convention Against Torture (Blau and Moncado 2009). But perhaps the moral power of the document, rather than the subsequent treaties that it helped generate, is more important. Indeed, the Universal Declaration has been awarded the Guinness Record for being the most translated document in the world, having been transcribed into 370 different languages and dialects (Guinness Records 2014). And it has provided a catalyst for human rights activism and advocacy around the world, from both large organizations with a global reach like **Amnesty International**, which specifically references the Universal Declaration in its mission statement, but also from smaller grassroots campaigns in particular countries around the world.

The rights enumerated in the Universal Declaration (please read in the Appendix) will be our starting place for a human rights approach to social problems. But when using the document, we will also be cognizant that the declaration is by no means a perfect or complete expression of human rights. As a social construction, it is a product of its time, and it is limited accordingly. Most importantly, when the Declaration was being drafted in 1948, much of Africa, Southeast Asia, and some of the Caribbean was still claimed as colonial territory by European nations. In this regard, **colonialism** structured who possessed human rights and who didn't. It is a striking limitation that, when being drafted, many people of Asian, African, and indigenous ancestry were excluded. Moreover, people then considered sexual dissidents (gays, lesbians, bisexuals) and impoverished rural peoples were also left out. And given that the Declaration was written before the environmental movement awakened people's awareness about the dire consequences of pollution and unrestrained resource use, rights to clean air, water, and other natural amenities were never considered.

Additionally, it is worth pointing out that rights may be contradictory, in that the complete granting of rights to one group of persons might be perceived as violating the rights of others. But the Declaration gives little advice on how such dilemmas may be resolved. For instance, some activists in the United States and Europe have campaigned against circumcising male infants, arguing that because it poses unnecessary health risks to babies, has few-to-no health benefits, and causes pain, it is a violation to the rights of children (Sardi 2011). On the other hand, circumcision is an important religious rite in both the Jewish and Islamic faiths. So when a German court recently placed restrictions on infant circumcision in the name of protecting the rights of children, it caused an uproar and raised concerns that the rights of groups to practice their own religion were being trammeled (Poggolio 2012). The Universal Declaration of Human Rights, of course, provides no instructions on how conflicting rights such as these might be negotiated.

The Universal Declaration of Human Rights is an imperfect and incomplete document. But it was never intended to be the final decree on all rights that any human group may claim. Rather, when it was written within its particular historic context, as the preamble of the document itself explains, it was intended to be a powerful call to action to make the world a better place for all of us who call it home. It was intended as a

> Common standard of achievement for all peoples and all nations, to the end that every individual and every organ of society, keeping this Declaration constantly in mind, shall strive by teaching and education to promote respect for these rights and freedoms and by progressive measures, national and international, to secure their universal and effective recognition and observance ...

Human rights, in other words, are the global framework by which contemporary individuals can evaluate their own society. By providing this framework, human rights become a basis from which individuals and groups can work to advance the human condition. So, while many people simply think of "human rights" as a set of international and often quite toothless treaties, we will think of them in a more expansive way, as a set of normative expectations that provide an impetus for social action for people around the world. But more than that, we will use an international human rights framework as a means to evaluate U.S. society.

When undertaking our evaluation, we will use the Universal Declaration of Human Rights as a starting place, while also recognizing that the document is necessarily incomplete and that human rights themselves are a project always "in the making." As we move forward, we will also consider what happens when rights are perceived to be contradictory, and how inequality and differences in **power** influence whose rights prevail over others. Finally, we will recognize that there is a utopian aspect to thinking about human rights, in the sense that the full granting of all the rights proclaimed in the Universal Declaration is likely impossibly far away for all the world's people. While this is true, it is certainly within our nation's capacity to fulfill rights much further for many more people than exists today. This is the work at hand for our particular historical era, there for us, if we should choose to take it up.

DISCUSSION QUESTIONS

1. Can you identify and describe examples of things you have been told are terrible problems, only to later realize that they weren't so bad after all? How might a constructionist perspective help us understand how this example of a "non-problem" social problem came into existence and gained popularity as a way to interpret the world?
2. Social constructionists take the position that no set of conditions is inherently problematic. Anything could potentially be interpreted as such, but this depends upon cultural and historical context. Do you agree? In contrast to social constructionism,

can you think of any conditions that might be inherently problematic? When thinking about your example, how do you know that you are not simply applying your own normative framework, which is specific to your own time and place?

3. Do you believe that the rights expressed in the Universal Declaration are an adequate articulation of our shared expectations of the things all people deserve and should be protected from in life? When looking over the document, are you personally willing to forgo any of these expectations for your own life? If you are personally unwilling to forgo any of these expectations, is it fair to say that others should be denied these rights?

4. The Universal Declaration of Human Rights is very much a product of its time. From our historical vantage point, do you think any of the rights it pronounces should be removed? Can you think of any rights that should be included if the member countries of the United Nations were, hypothetically, to update the document?

Note

1 The eight countries that abstained from voting were the Soviet Union and five aligned communist nations (the Ukrainian Soviet Socialist Republic, the Byelorussian Soviet Socialist Republic, Poland, Yugoslavia, and Czechoslovakia), along with South Africa and the Kingdom of Saudi Arabia (Morsink 1999).

II: Rights to Wellbeing and Property in an Unequal Society

～～✕～～

On September 17, 2011 protesters literally moved into Zuccotti Park, in New York City's Wall Street financial district, in order to maintain an ongoing demonstration. The act inspired thousands of other protests, as young people "occupied" public spaces in other major American cities like Oakland, California, but also in such far-flung places as tiny Casper, Wyoming and Fairbanks, Alaska (CBS 2011). While the goals of the protestors were many, the most notable accomplishment of the movement was to raise awareness of American inequality. One of the inspirations from the protest movement was a blog entitled *We Are The 99 Percent*, in which users posted a picture of themselves (though their faces were often obstructed to not fully disclose their identity) along with stories of the economic plight they faced. Stories such as these read:

> I quit high school when I was 17 to work more hours in a pharmacy to help my Mom. Now I'm 21 and I just lost the only job I've ever known and w/it, my health insurance. Even though I am a certified pharmacy tech, there is no work for me. I may have to quit college to work anywhere just to make ends meet. Bills keep pilling up and I have no idea how I'll pay them.
>
> (99 Percent 2011a)

> I am 32. I have 2 college degrees. I worked earning both. I am in debt $25k for them. I make $30k a year, but have to pay $260 a month for health insurance … I paid my bills. I have 26 cents until payday. My co-workers are the same … We all work 50–60 hrs. a week minimum, no OT [overtime] because we are salaried. I feel like a failure.
>
> (99 Percent 2011b)

> I went to school to pursue my dreams. I am now $10,000 in debt with an associates degree, and cannot find work. I am again financially dependent on my struggling parents. I feel like a failure. I hate that my talents are going to waste.
>
> (99 Percent 2011c)

These representative stories on the *We Are The 99 percent* blog indicate that when we use an international human rights framework to evaluate U.S. society, we see that our own nation falls short in many important ways (Armaline, Glasberg, and Purkayastha 2011). Some of the greatest insufficiencies in the contemporary United States have to do with rights to wellbeing. If you look back at the Universal Declaration of Human Rights again, our list of shared expectations about what people deserve in life and what they should be protected from, you'll not only see calls for the guarantee of rights to the material conditions necessary for life, but also calls for the right to a life with dignity, for adequate healthcare, and accessible education. In this chapter, we will examine U.S. society in regard to these rights, and try to answer why it is that these rights go unfilled for so many people within one of the most wealthy nations on the planet.

Dignity and Wellbeing Compromised

Imagine a family in your community that is comprised of a parent and two children who live on an income of $25,000 a year, which works out to approximately $1,900 per month after payroll taxes. After paying $1,000 in rent for a modest one-bedroom apartment, the family has $900 for food, clothing, medicine, toiletries, transportation, and childcare. The question is then, after paying for rent, is this income sufficient to pay for all the things that are required for a life of dignity in the United States? This hypothetical family is representative of hundreds of thousands of real families across the country. Are its members poor? When answering this question, it is necessary to account for the all the expenses that a family might have in order to be comfortable and to be deemed "normal" in the United States. For instance, after paying for the essentials, is there money left over to buy nice-looking clothes for the children from time to time? Is there money left over for the dentist in order to make sure that the kids have healthy teeth that don't develop painful cavities, which left untreated can diminish the children's quality of life? Is there money left over for school sports and fieldtrips, for which underfunded schools are increasingly asking parents to pay? Finally, is the food that is purchased for these kids full of the more expensive fruits and vegetables we know are important for a healthy diet, or can this parent only afford the highly processed, high-fat foods that are cheaper, but are also associated with the development of obesity and diabetes?

Depending on how one defines a "necessity" and how one answers these questions, we might say that this family is poor, and that poverty constitutes a serious social problem that compromises human dignity. The human rights of these children, in other words—like those of millions of other children in the United States—are not being adequately met. While *we* might find the children in such families to be poor—using a **relative measure of poverty** that considers if a family's earnings are sufficient to provide a life of dignity in a given society—this family would not be counted officially poor by the U.S. government. In fact, this family lives on an income that is much higher—$6,500 more, to be exact—than the official threshold the U.S. government uses to measure poverty.

When the U.S. government assesses poverty, it uses an **absolute measure**, which has to do with the lack of the material conditions—food, clean water, clothing, shelter—that are necessary for life. The official U.S. threshold was first determined using an estimate of the average cost of a nutritionally adequate diet, depending upon family size, and then multiplying it by three to account for other crucial household expenses such as housing, clothes, healthcare, and transportation (Fisher 1997). Using these calculations, the **U.S. Census Bureau** conducts surveys to measure how many people live on annual incomes—before taxes, but not including forms of non-cash assistance like food stamps or housing vouchers—that are less than the official poverty threshold.

In 2012, the official poverty threshold was set at just less than $12,000 for an individual, or $18,500 for a family consisting of a parent and two children. In 2011, 46.2 million people lived on annual incomes below these levels, meaning that 15 percent of all Americans lived below the official poverty rate (DeNavas-Walt, Proctor, and Smith 2012). More troubling still, almost 22 percent of children in the United States, or more than one in five kids, live in families whose income is below the official poverty line (DeNavas-Walt, Proctor, and Smith 2012). The extent of poverty in the United States constitutes an obvious collective failure to live up to the standards outlined in the Universal Declaration.

And as high as these numbers are, many sociologists, policy experts, and Congressional legislators argue that they underestimate poverty in the United States (Heiner 2012; Short 2013). For one, much has changed in the U.S. economy since 1965 when the official poverty threshold measure was first developed. Family expenses for childcare and healthcare, for example, have increased dramatically since then. And a measure developed in 1965 is obviously unable to account for the expense of a computer and internet connection that many people deem essential to raise educated and well-prepared children. Moreover, the Census Bureau does not account for the ways that the cost of living differs depending upon location in the lower 48 states. Housing and food are much more expensive in some places compared to others, especially in some large American cities, where those living at even 200 percent of the poverty line may be challenged to survive. The Census Bureau has developed new measures of poverty, such as the Supplemental Poverty Measure, that unlike the current measure, are not based on extrapolations of the cost of food decades go, but instead determine a threshold based upon the cost of important family expenses like healthcare and childcare, while also accounting for some forms of public assistance as forms of income (Short 2013). Such new thresholds, however, are yet to be fully institutionalized. Perhaps this is because it is politically expedient to underestimate the extent of poverty in the United States (Heiner 2012). If our official measure of poverty showed even greater amounts of destitution across the country than the current measure shows, after all, people might be more likely to demand that changes be made.

Beyond the extent of poverty itself, many other rights proclaimed in the Universal Declaration go unfulfilled in the United States, including the right to work. In 2013, the official U.S. unemployment rate was above 7 percent, but this too is an underestimate. The U.S. Bureau of Labor Statistics determines this number through telephone surveys, where persons are counted as employed if they did any work in the past week for pay, even if for just a few hours. It also does not count persons as unemployed if they did not actively apply for a job in the past four weeks (BLS 2013). In reality, a person who only works a few hours per week, say doing yard work for a neighbor or doing a day's temporary work at a factory, should probably be considered unemployed because he or she is not earning an adequate income to live on and most likely yearns for a regular job. And people who have dropped out of the workforce altogether, after having given up after spending months looking for a job with no luck, should really be counted as unemployed too. But because the official unemployment statistics leave these individuals out, the final tabulation underestimates the extent of joblessness in the United States. The figures can tell us something about the relative health of the economy, but in terms of human wellbeing in the United States, they need to be taken with a grain of salt. However we count them, tens of millions of Americans are regularly denied work, an important human right in contemporary society.

Related to these bread and butter issues of work and income, the Universal Declaration insists that all people should have access to healthcare and access to higher education. Though Americans cannot legally be turned away from emergency medical care, the increasing costs of healthcare over the past several decades have—even with insurance—priced many low- and moderate-income Americans out of the market for the kinds of preventative medical care that can enhance the quality of life and, ultimately, help people live longer. The high cost of medical care is an important reason why, despite having some of the most advanced medical technology in the world, the United States does not compare favorably to other wealthy nations in important measures of health. Sociologists often use comparative analyses to understand how one country differs from another. For example, while the average person in the tiny country of Monaco can expect to live to be almost 90, and a person in Japan has a good chance of living to 84, life-expectancy in the United States is far lower at only 79 (CIA 2013a). Infant mortality is another important measure where the United States does not excel, being a measure of the number of deaths within one year of life per 1,000 babies born. The United States ranks just barely ahead of nations like Croatia and Slovakia in regard to infant mortality, and just behind other countries like Greece and Cuba (CIA 2013b). In terms of access to higher education, another wellbeing right, the steadily rising costs of college over the past several decades, as you might well know, make obtaining an advanced degree a real struggle for many students today, saddling millions with student loan debt they will be paying off for decades and preventing some would-be students from attending college altogether. Taking all this together, it's clear that U.S. society fails to provide wellbeing rights for all its citizens. The next section will consider some policy alternatives that could make life better for millions throughout our nation.

Achieving Wellbeing for All in U.S. Society

In 1964 the Food Stamp Act was passed in order to provide public support to low-income Americans in order to eliminate hunger and malnutrition. Since that time, it has literally been a lifeline for many Americans in these tough economic times. In 2012, the Food Stamp Program's replacement—the Supplemental Nutrition Assistance Program (or **SNAP**) provided almost $80 billion in food support. Even so, the average daily benefit is only $4.30, which falls far short of providing a healthy diet for most Americans—including millions of children—in need. SNAP could be improved to ensure that the food it provides is full of the nutritious fresh ingredients necessary for health. Some communities, for instance, have had real success partnering with local farmers to get fresh produce to those on SNAP, as well as making it more accessible to other low-income earners who might find it otherwise unaffordable (Boyd 2013). There is no reason why, at least technically speaking, these programs couldn't be scaled up to a national level (Agyeman 2013).

The **Head Start** program, begun in 1965, now provides preschool education to almost a million children every year whose families could not otherwise afford it. It plays an important role in U.S. society by enabling children from poor families to enter school at similar reading levels as their their middle-class peers, making sure poor kids don't get behind in primary school before they even begin (Rich 2012). There have been calls to make Head Start available to all four-year-olds from low- and moderate-income families, most recently in a presidential State of the Union address (Obama 2013). But other nations do not stop at providing public funding to preschool and K-12 schooling when educating upcoming generations. New Zealand and many European nations provide much more substantial support to students in college, making the costs students pay to attend just a small fraction of the price of an advanced degree in the United States (Taylor 2012). And of course, we know that practically all other wealthy nations provide universal health coverage to their citizens, something that further promotes wellbeing rights for all.

One major reason the needs of the poor remain unaddressed in the United States is due to lack of employment, which is considered a right in and of itself in the Universal Declaration. Unemployment is a durable feature of capitalism, but economic downturns and other trends (such as **globalization** and **automation**, which we will explore in other chapters) can make it much worse. In the Great Depression of the 1930s, the federal government sought to curb unemployment and promote economic growth by employing millions of workers through the Works Progress Administration—which built roads, bridges, schools, and libraries across the nation—and through the Civilian Conservation Corps—which created many buildings and roads in our national and state parks that are still used today (Taylor 2008). These programs built some of the key infrastructure that helped fuel economic growth in subsequent decades. But perhaps more importantly, when these programs gave millions of Americans jobs, it also provided them money that could pay the bills but—just as importantly—a sense of dignity and self-worth that was in tatters from the effects of the Depression (Taylor 2008).

Similarly, Van Jones (2008), a former member of Obama's presidential administration and a leading American environmental justice advocate, argues that the U.S. government could step in today to provide jobs to those who need and want work, but who are nonetheless unable to find employment in the private sector. Like the New Deal, this new jobs program would again build the infrastructure necessary to spur future economic growth, but this time the focus would be on a greener and more sustainable U.S. economy. Members of this new "green collar" jobs program could, for instance be trained and paid to retrofit homes and apartments to make them more energy efficient, to build a high-speed rail transit system across the country—as already exists in Japan, China, and Europe—or by building solar panel or wind-turbine systems to generate clean electricity (Jones 2008).

While government programs to promote wellbeing in the United States might sound nice as ideas, we are often told that in reality they are hopelessly impractical, especially given our nation's current fiscal constraints. These programs, "experts" often say, are simply too unaffordable. The next section considers the extent to which this is true.

Concentrations of Wealth and Power in the United States

The United States has by far and away the largest economy in the world. When we divvy up the size of the economy based on population, in a measure called per capita gross domestic product, and compare the United States to the rest of the world, we see that while it is not number one on the list, it is very close to the top, and that the U.S. economy maintains a position that is the envy of most of the world. But averages can be misleading. Benefits from the U.S. economy are distributed very unequally. One way to measure inequality is the Gini index, which ranks the distribution of family incomes in a nation. Based on this index, the United States is a highly unequal nation, with an income distribution on par with other countries like Jamaica, Cameroon, and the Philippines, as you can see in Table 2.1.

Income distribution is one way to measure income inequality. You can see on the graph in Figure 2.1 that the poorest 20 percent, or bottom quintile, of the U.S.

Table 2.1 Inequality by Nation (Ranked Most to Least Unequal)

Rank	Country	Gini Index
1	Lesotho	63
2	South Africa	63
3	Botswana ↓↑	63
40	Uruguay	45
41	U.S.A	45
42	Philippines ↓↑	45
134	Montenegro	24
135	Slovenia	24
136	Sweden	23

Source: *CIA World Factbook* (CIA 2013c).

population earns only 3 percent of the nation's total income. The top earning 20 percent of the population, on the other hand, earns just over 50 percent of all income for that year. The richest 5 percent make an even more disproportionate share, earning more than 21 percent of America's income total (DeNavas-Walt, Proctor, and Smith 2012). But the higher we go in America's economic echelons, the greater the inequality. The chief financial officers of major corporations earn several hundred times more than the average salary of their U.S. workers, as Table 2.2 shows. In 2012, for instance, Oracle CEO Larry Ellison earned $96.2 million in just one year, which is 1,287 times the average pay for U.S. workers in the electronics/technology sector (Blair-Smith and Kuntz 2013).

But rather than looking at income, a better way to assess economic inequality is by looking at **wealth**, which is the sum total of everything a person owns (including

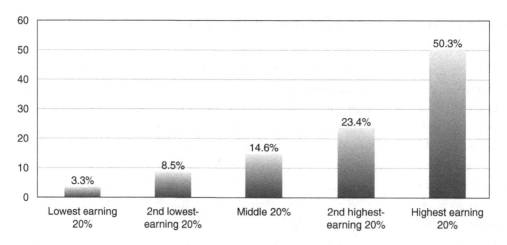

Figure 2.1 Share of National Income by Quintile

Source: U.S. Census Bureau (2012) *Income, Poverty, and Health Coverage in the United States: 2011.*

Table 2.2 Compensation of Selected CEOs Compared to Average Worker Compensation per Industry

CEO	Company	Compensation (2012)	Average Employee Compensation in Industry (2012)
Lawrence Ellison	Oracle Corp.	$96.2 million	$75,000
Michael Jeffries	Abercrombie & Fitch Co.	$48.1 million	$29,000
Robert Iger	Walt Disney Co.	$40.2 million	$66,000
Rupert Murdoch	News Corp.	$33.5 million	$66,000
Howard Schultz	Starbucks Corp.	$28.9 million	$25,000

Source: Blair-Smith and Kuntz (2013) "Top CEO Pay Ratios."

property, stocks, bonds, business ventures, and money in the bank) minus debts (home loans, credit card debt, college loans, etc.). After all, income can come and go, even for relatively high earners who might live paycheck to paycheck. But wealth is significant because it can produce income, because it can provide an important "cushion" during economic hard times and—most importantly—because it is a form of inequality that can be handed down between generations (Conley 1999; Shapiro and Oliver 1997). As we can see in Figure 2.2, the great majority of Americans have no, or only very little, wealth. The least wealthy 50 percent of Americans own only 1 percent of the nation's total wealth. And most of that is bound up in home ownership. In contrast, the wealthiest 1 percent of Americans posses 35 percent of everything that can be owned in the nation, while those in the next wealthiest 9 percent hold another 40 percent of all wealth (Mishel 2012). It is important to remember that wealth is often inherited, and once wealth is inherited, it can be used to produce more wealth. One analysis of members of the *Forbes 400* richest Americans found that while 35 percent came from middle-class and lower-class backgrounds, the rest were members

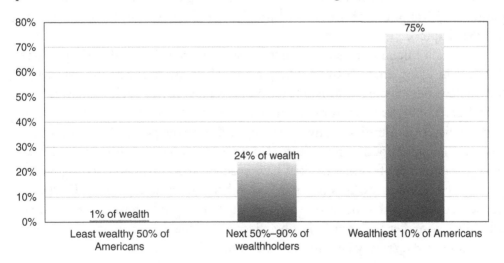

Figure 2.2 Distribution of Wealth (2010)

Source: Mishel (2012) "Confirming the Further Upward Distribution of Wealth."

of families that possessed significantly more wealth than the average American when they began life (United for a Fair Economy 2012).

We might consider the story of Sam Walton, for instance, who was something of a "self-made man." As the founder of Wal-Mart, he became the wealthiest person in America. When he died, however, he left billions to his wife and children, who are now each worth more than $25 billion and are ranked six through nine on the *Forbes* list of the richest Americans (*Forbes* 2012). As an interesting side note, the Walton heirs' combined wealth is equivalent to the total wealth owned by the bottom 48 percent (or 150 million) of the least wealthy Americans (Bivens 2012). All of this is to say that there are financial resources to provide for the increased fulfillment of wellbeing rights in America. Lack of money is not the issue, it is more a matter of priorities and power.

It is important to understand that the American **social structure** is built on the foundations of capitalism, which is an economic system of immensely productive potential and one that promotes continuous technological innovation. It is also one, however, that tends to concentrate wealth over time and produces increasing economic inequality both within and between nations. This trend is not necessarily inevitable, however, because governments can intervene with tax, educational, and welfare policies to promote greater equality. We know that this is true because we can look at examples from other capitalist nations or even by looking at U.S. society during different historical periods. There is a long line of economic thinking that even argues that such government intervention to diminish inequality is a good thing for capitalism because it promotes stability and ensures that the vast majority of would-be consumers have enough money to actually purchase the products that companies make and sell. Efforts to institute governmental policies to promote greater equality are hindered, however, by a worldview, or **ideology**, in America that tends to celebrate wealth while overlooking the suffering of the poor, along with the substantial political power of the richest Americans (which we will further consider in the next chapter).

If there is such thing as one single American worldview, it is one that simply can't "see" the plight of low-income and working people. For instance, when the stories of the top 52 news outlets were indexed for the past several years, an analysis showed that less than 1 percent of the news stories each year were about poverty (Froomkin 2013). Even in our own communities, many Americans rarely see the poor, who typically live in different neighborhoods and whose children often go to different schools. Increasingly, a number of American cities have enacted codes that ban loitering, sleeping, and panhandling in parks, sidewalks, and other public spaces (NLCHP 2011). While these codes are often couched in terms of protecting public health, the outcome of such policies—either by intention or by effect—is to make homelessness and poverty less visible in the areas where they are enforced.

While Americans have little capacity to learn about the plight of the poor from the daily news, movies, or television shows that they watch, they can learn a great deal about how to celebrate wealth and material success. Americans are constantly taught that everyone should have it. And because success and fortune are depicted in American media as obtainable for the smart and the hardworking, the lesson is that the poor have themselves to blame. This is hardly a cultural context that is conducive to satisfying wellbeing rights, especially if doing so is seen to impinge on the right to possess all those material riches in the first place.

Since the 1980s there has been a concerted effort in the United States to roll back social spending on the poor. This endeavor has been led by a number of think tanks and political organizations, including the Heritage Society, the American Enterprise Institute, and—perhaps most successfully—Americans for Tax Reform. This latter group, for instance, mounted a campaign in 1985 to convince politicians to pledge that they will not raise taxes. The campaign was tremendously effective, by 2011 almost 95 percent of the Republican members of Congress had signed on (Horowitz 2011). These organizations portray assistance to the poor not in terms of human rights, but often as wasteful and unnecessary expenditures of everybody else's money. What's more, these organizations typically portray taxation as a violation of peoples' right to their possessions. The result is that in the face of a fairly large government debt, politicians in the United States—as in some European countries—have sought to institute policies of **austerity**, or rollbacks on public spending, rather than increasing taxes on the well-to-do. This means that, in the United States, the social support system that provides for basic human rights for the poor through programs that offer cash assistance, which has become increasingly meager and non-existent in some states—food stamps, preschool, medical care, and housing subsidies—have come under constant attack and have been increasingly whittled down in the past years.

The right to property certainly is a fundamental right in the contemporary era, proclaimed in the Universal Declaration, which practically no serious person today wants to abolish. But at the same time, this right can't be absolute in contemporary societies either. In modern economies, wealth is achieved through complex networks of dependency that span entire regions, in many cases even the whole globe (as we will see in Chapter VI). The Wal-Mart heirs' fortune, after all, was not just built by one individual man who constructed department stores around the country, but also by the cities that often subsidized the development of those stores, by the consumers who had enough disposable income to buy products there, and by the federal government that provided the food stamps and healthcare that sustain many of the Wal-Mart workers who are paid wages so low that they qualify for these programs (Fox 2013). In this sense, no one's fortune is entirely self-made. It is for this reason that the Universal Declaration of Rights notes, near its end, that societies do not only grant rights to individuals, they also obligate individuals to respect the rights of others. There has to be, in other words, a way to balance the tension between the rights to wellbeing and the right to property in the United States.

Striking a Balance Between Property Ownership and Wellbeing to Satisfy Rights

In the United States, we have said, government policies tend to disproportionately favor the rights to property of the few over the wellbeing rights for all. This, we have said, is due both to our American worldview that celebrates material success while ignoring poverty and misfortune, along with the political mobilization of the very wealthy. This may be an example of a more general rule in regard to human rights: when there is friction between the satisfaction of rights between two groups—that is when the granting of rights to one group is seen as diminishing the rights of another— then we should expect that the group with the greater amount of social power will prevail in political contests over their fulfillment. In the United States, members of the wealthiest ranks of our society are typically very politically active, contributing money to both political candidates and to think tanks and other political organizations that fight for low taxes and diminished public services (Domhoff 2009). And they have been, in the past several decades, by and large very successful. But thinking about this rule means we don't have to accept our contemporary situation in the United States as inevitable. If lower-income and less wealthy Americans were to become more politically active, there is no reason why a new balance could not be struck between satisfying both rights to property *and* rights to wellbeing in the United States. Here are a few ideas about how that might look.

One obvious place to begin would be to dramatically increase the estate tax, which is levied on large inheritances when they are passed down to the next generation. In 2013, the estate tax is levied on only a small percentage of Americans, those passing on an inheritance of more than $5.25 million. The inheritance is taxed at a top rate of 35 percent, but only on any amount of money beyond this $5.25 million exemption. The estate tax in the United States, however, was once much more hefty, with a higher top rate of 77 percent and a much smaller exemption set at $60,000 between 1942 and 1976 (*Cook and Cook* 2012). Accounting for inflation, this exemption varies between $246,000 (in 1976) and $900,000 (in 1942) in 2013 dollars, depending upon the particular year in question. Going back to these historic levels of estate taxes, or even taxing inherited wealth at higher rates, could provide an important source of revenue for funding programs to provision wellbeing rights in the United States.

Doing so could be an important way to balance rights between property and wellbeing. While Americans might claim a right to wealth earned in their lifetimes, do they have an inviolable right to pass that wealth on to their kids? Our current system of inheritance means that the heirs of the very wealthy are lifted far up above others in their generation only because they happened to be born lucky, while it also means that the less fortunate children of others go without a healthy diet and access to preschool. Is this the best balance between the rights to property and wellbeing we can find? It is of course not surprising that socialists like Karl Marx wholeheartedly disagree, arguing that the inheritances of the very wealthy could have a higher social value than being passed on in great concentrations to heirs and heiresses. But other critics of wealth inheritance come from less obvious places. Andrew Carnegie, for instance, was a 19th-century steel magnate who became one of America's most wealthy men. He was, in other words, about as far away from a socialist and as big a booster of capitalism as you can get. At the same time, he was a supporter of high taxes on inherited wealth, writing that, "of all forms of taxation, this seems the wisest ... By taxing estates heavily at death, the state marks its condemnation of the selfish millionaire's unworthy life." Going on, Carnegie wrote, "the more society is organized around the preservation of wealth for those who already have it, rather than building new wealth, the more impoverished we will all be" (quoted in Miller 2004: 116). One of the most successful businessmen in our era, Warren Buffett, seems to agree. He has said that he "doesn't believe in dynastic wealth," calling those who gained their fortunes from their parents, "members of the lucky sperm club" (quoted in Thomas 2006). Both Buffett and billionaire Microsoft founder Bill Gates have pledged to give away the vast majority of their wealth before they die.

Buffett has also been an outspoken critic of today's tax rate on "capital gains," or the income generated through wealth. In the United States, capital gains are taxed at 15 percent, which is much less than the effective rate paid by middle-class Americans on their income taxes. The consequence is that, according to Buffett (2011), "if you earn money from a job, your [tax] percentage will surely exceed mine, most likely by a lot." Under this current system, in other words, wealthy individuals who live on profits returned from investments—perhaps most famously like 2012 presidential candidate Mitt Romney, whose low tax rate became an issue in the race—pay less as a percentage of their earnings compared to the vast majority of Americans who earn a living through a paycheck. The tax rate on capital gains could of course be increased, and this could provide another possible means of paying for programs that could better fulfill the wellbeing rights of Americans.

These are just two ideas of ways that the tensions between the rights to property and wellbeing might be negotiated in U.S. society. But possibilities abound, such as the **living wage** codes that have been enacted in a number of cities across the United States, which require businesses that have contracts with, or receive subsidies from, the municipality to pay employees a wage sufficient for housing, a healthy diet, healthcare, and childcare costs. In other words, these codes mean that in order to do business with or receive benefits from such cities, companies must pay a wage that can fulfill the wellbeing rights of workers. When cities consider enacting such policies, however, they are frequently told that businesses can't afford to pay living wages, and that requiring them to do so will curtail employment and slow growth (Lester and Jacobs 2010). But this is a dubious claim. A study of 31 cities showed, for instance, that neither employment nor growth were curtailed when city lawmakers put a living wage code on their books (Lester and Jacobs 2010). Perhaps living wage codes could be enacted more broadly as a means of promoting the wellbeing rights of workers, something college students around the country have been working to accomplish on their own campuses since the mid-1990s with some success.

The point of this exercise is to make clear that, while U.S. society favors property rights over rights to wellbeing, this doesn't necessarily have to be the case. We are often told that there is no money for increased spending to address poverty, especially in these times of austerity and government debt. But we see from the examples provided in this chapter that funding is available if there is political will to change existing policies. None of the policy alternatives offered here disregard the right to property, but they do make some increased demands on business owners or the wealthy in order to more fully satisfy wellbeing rights. Increasing the estate tax or capital gains tax does not, seek to eliminate wealth. And city living wage codes don't require businesses to pay living wages at all—although this might be a good idea—but they do require any company that *chooses* to do business with or receive a subsidy from a city to pay employees a wage adequate for a life with dignity. Such efforts, of course, will be, and have been, contested by many Americans who do not want to see any limits placed on their capacity to possess wealth. The estate tax, for instance, has been maligned by organizations funded by wealthy donors as a "death tax." These organizations have sought to achieve—with some success, as we've seen—its repeal. This brings us to an important lesson: human rights are not just about what is just and unjust in a particular society, but about the balance of power between groups. A balance of power can change over time toward the increased fulfillment of human rights, but this doesn't just happen on its own, it has much to do with the efforts of large numbers of people organizing and working together to make it so.

DISCUSSION QUESTIONS

1. Do you think poverty is made invisible in the United States? In the rare instances when we do have discussions about poverty and unemployment, do you think the less fortunate are blamed for their condition? Please give examples when you explain why or why not.

2. How might inheriting wealth make a difference to a family's economic prospects? Imagine two families with kids just barely getting by on their income. One family inherits $10,000 and the other does not. What kinds of new opportunities—home ownership, college tuition, etc.—might be opened up for this family that remain closed for the other?

3. This chapter made the case that governments play an important role promoting wellbeing rights, and some ideas were presented to suggest ways that the U.S. government might do better. Did any of these ideas capture your imagination and seem especially important? Did any seem unworkable and/or ineffective? Explain why or why not.

4. While we are often told that there is simply no money to provide for the increased wellbeing of poor and low-income persons in the United States, this chapter argued that more revenue can be found by increasing the taxation of wealth or by requiring companies to pay their employees living wages. Do you think this is fair? Should those with large amounts of wealth be asked to pay more to promote broader wellbeing in America? If you answer no, what do you think are the best alternatives?

III: American Inequality and the Rights to Speech and Democracy

~~~~~~~~~

The political beliefs of David and Charles Koch (pronounced *coke*) may not be extraordinary, but the amount of money these two brothers are willing to spend on politics certainly is. In 2012, the two brothers pledged to spend $60 million to unseat Obama in his reelection battle and to otherwise pursue libertarian causes (Terkel and Grim 2012). The exact amount of money they spent is not clear because much of it was funneled into political organizations that are not required to disclose their contributions. But from what political analysts can gather, the total was certainly in the tens of millions (Gilson 2012). Perhaps more consequentially, these brothers have spent at least $100 million elsewhere to fund libertarian think tanks and build the libertarian-leaning "Tea Party" movement (Mayer 2010). But maybe there's no problem with this amount of political spending. Aren't these two brothers, who happen to be among the top 10 richest Americans, simply enjoying their human rights to free speech and democratic participation?

U.S. citizens, after all, firmly believe in the importance of free speech and the idea that all people have a right to meaningfully participate and have influence within our various levels of government. Free speech is guaranteed in the First Amendment of the Bill of Rights, and the notion of a right to democratic participation is perhaps even more fundamental, being a quintessential way Americans understand themselves. Mostly, we think of these rights as complementary. By having the right to political speech, after all, Americans often presume that if they have something important to say, others will listen. If enough of these other individuals agree with what is said, the story we like to tell ourselves goes, politicians will listen to this speech as well and will enact corresponding changes to law and policy. These politicians, after all, are dependent upon votes from members of the public, so they had better do what the public wants or they risk losing their jobs. This is the idea of **pluralism**: everyone's speech is protected, and everyone's speech is, hypothetically, equally influential depending upon what's being said. The right to speech and the right to participate in one's government go hand in hand.

Unfortunately, as we will see in this chapter, things get messy in very unequal societies like our own. The U.S. Supreme Court has consistently interpreted campaign spending as a form of free speech, making this case most forcefully in the 2010 decision *Citizens United vs. FEC*. But if money in politics is considered a kind of speech, what happens when a few individuals have vast amounts of money on hand to spend, which isn't available to others? This chapter will show that the predictable result is that the democratic rights of the majority of Americans are undermined. In a very unequal society like ours, rights to speech and democratic participation are not just complementary, they are potentially contradictory as well. To consider this argument, we will first examine the role of political contributions in today's electoral campaigns. We will then consider how this money distorts the relationship between candidates, elected officials, and voters. Finally, we'll close by considering some possible ways that rights to speech and democratic rights might be better balanced, something which would improve governance in the United States and likely increase the public's participation within the political process.

Running for Office in America (It Takes Millions)

Just how much money does it cost to run for public office in the United States? The answer is a whole lot, especially if we are taking about national office. As we can see in Table 3.1, running for public office was an expensive proposition indeed in the 2012 election cycle, costing candidates for the U.S. House almost $1.5 million, candidates for the Senate almost $10 million, while President Obama's campaign alone raised more than $775 million. When collecting this money, of course, candidates must ask donors to conform to national campaign finance limits. In 2013, a person was limited to giving $2,600 per candidate per election cycle. This is, undoubtedly, far more money than most people could afford to contribute, no matter how much they want their candidate to win. But, for more well-to-do Americans, there are ways to legally give beyond these initial limits, for instance by giving to a candidate both in a primary and during a regular election—effectively doubling the total contribution. And if this wealthy patron is married, he or she could convince a spouse to give at this limit as well, doubling the contribution again. What's more, wealthy supporters can give up to $32,400 to national political parties, which can then use this money to campaign on behalf of the individual candidate.

But for the past couple of decades, some wealthy Americans have found even these very generous levels to be far too restricting. Consequently, they have also put money into **political action committees** and, increasingly, into 501(c)4 "**social welfare groups**" to campaign on behalf of an elected official. This outside spending, at more than one billion dollars in the 2012 election cycle alone, fuels campaigns above and beyond the amounts reflected in Table 3.1. For instance, outside groups, many of which do not have to disclose the names of their contributors at the time of an election, if disclosure is required at all, ended up spending several hundred million dollars on behalf of both the 2012 presidential candidates. In fact, outside spending by groups supporting candidate Mitt Romney almost equaled the total amount raised by the

Table 3.1 Average Amount of Money Raised by Winners per Office, 2012 Elections

Office	Party	Average Amount Raised
House	Republicans	$1,734, 000
	Democrats	$1,665,000
Senate	Republicans	$8,064,000
	Democrats	$11,567,000
President	Democrat (Obama)	$715,678,000

Source: Center for Responsive Politics (2013a and b) "Price of Admission" and "2012 Presidential Race."

campaign itself, which collected individual contributions governed by federal spending limits (CRP 2013b).

By giving to outside groups, wealthy individuals can give millions of dollars in hopes of influencing elections. In 2012, for instance, the developer and casino owner Sheldon Adelson and his wife gave $93 million, while Harold and Annette Simmons gave almost $28 million, and New York mayor Michael Bloomberg gave almost $14 million of his own money to fund campaigns (CRP 2013c). Our political system is no doubt awash in money, but the question is, does it matter?

How Money in Politics Undermines Democratic Rights

To be clear, most of the money raised by candidates for national office in the United States comes from large donations, those that are over $200 in size. What's more, only a tiny fraction of Americans are making donations this large, less than one half of one percent (0.4 percent) of the total population (CRP 2013d). The money that drives political campaigns, in other words, comes largely from the relatively wealthy few Americans that can afford to donate it. But those that think pluralism is a good way to see and understand America's political system aren't too concerned with this state of affairs. After all, they argue, wealthy individuals back both Democratic and Republican candidates. And wealthy funders have a range of personal political interests, for example some are pro-life and some are pro-choice, while some are in favor of restrictions on the sale of firearms and some are not. And wealthy funders also have a range of different business interests: for instance some come from money in oil and coal and want to see fewer environmental restrictions, while others back clean energy technologies and want to see more rules reducing pollution. To pluralists, then, all this money just cancels itself out and is therefore not something worth worrying about at all.

Others, however, are not nearly so sanguine and believe that political candidates' need for donations from wealthy supporters distorts our nation's political process. Money by no means guarantees an election victory; more money was spent campaigning for Mitt Romney over that spent for Obama, for instance, but he still lost.

Nonetheless, having more money certainly helps. The ability to raise and spend more campaign money is seen as a tremendous advantage for political candidates. In 2012, for example, the winners of U.S. House seats raised on average three times the amount of their opponents (CRP 2013e). Part of this has to do with the "incumbent advantage." Candidates who are working to be reelected have a much greater ability to raise money, and consequently they are much more likely to maintain their seats after having once won. In 2012, incumbents won 90 percent of their congressional races (CRP 2012).

Politicians know that the more money they have, the greater chance they have of winning. This profoundly influences the ways that politicians spend their time, and creates the first distortion in the U.S. political system we will discuss. Americans might like to think that their members of Congress will continue to take the time to hear from their constituents once elected, and will work diligently to learn about the significant issues facing the nation. We Americans might like to think of members of Congress working to craft elegant policies based on what they learn, and putting in the significant amount of time necessary to forge compromises across the aisle. And while our Congress members might do some of these things while in office, we also know that they allocate a substantial amount of time to fundraising for the next election. Members of the House, for instance, are up for election every two years, meaning they need to raise about $1.5 million during that period on average to keep their seats. The amount of time they spend fundraising, however, means they have less time to do the important legislative work they were elected to accomplish in the first place.

Elected officials' reliance upon contributions from the wealthy creates yet another kind of distortion in the U.S. political system, which legal scholar Lawrence Lessig (2011) calls **institutional corruption**. Lessig believes that **personal corruption** has been a real problem in America's political system, which involves the quid pro quo exchange of money for political favors. Political scandals erupt from time to time, letting us know that this form of corruption is still around. But Lessig argues it is probably at an all-time low. More pressing, he believes, is the entirely legal form of corruption that permeates today's political environment, in which members of Congress give more access and attention to wealthy contributors compared to everyone else. This form of corruption may be more subtle than personal corruption, but in today's system it is far more corrosive.

Institutional corruption operates through a system of both dependency and fear. If an elected official has received a large contribution from one wealthy person, it is certainly reasonable to assume that he or she is going to be more willing to meet with this contributor and give a more sympathetic hearing to his or her concerns compared to those constituents who do not have the capacity to give a large contribution. Lessig (2011) compares this to the example of a drug company that pays a doctor to give talks recommending one of its brands of medicine. The doctor's talks are based on his or her professional and independent opinion. But at the same time, if the doctor wants to continue receiving the money the drug company is giving, then he or she better continue making the same recommendations or the paid talks will quickly come to an end. There is nothing illegal about this relationship of influence, but still the influence is there. In regard to the situation for the member of Congress, his or her relationship of dependency upon wealthy contributors is characterized by a hefty dose of fear. Such wealthy backers, after all, do not only have the power to discontinue their financial support, they can also promise to spend money to support the opponent of that candidate in the next election if things don't go their way.

Perhaps very large campaign contributions distort American politics in an even more fundamental way by influencing who can effectively run for office in the first place. Sociologist William Domhoff (2009) argues that Americans have their choices severely constrained by the time they get to cast their ballots in an election or even in a primary. Because raising large sums of money is so important in running for office in America's contemporary campaign finance environment, only those individuals who show fundraising promise are considered "serious" candidates. But because this money mostly comes from the very wealthy segments of U.S. society, it also means that the only "serious" candidates are the ones able to garner elite support. Those individuals, in both the Republican and Democratic parties, who do not say the things that potential wealthy backers most want to hear, will be effectively cast out of the race. So while Domhoff (2009) does not discount the idea that there can be some important differences between Democratic and Republican candidates, by the time of the general election Domhoff also thinks that these candidates—all having proved worthy of support from wealthy backers—will also be on the same page on a number of important issues.

These three distortions we have discussed undermine democratic rights. When Americans elect a person to Congress, they hope he or she will quickly get to the serious legislative work at hand, not immediately begin fundraising for the next election. And they certainly don't regard it as fair, in a representative democracy, when elected officials place the interests and needs of wealthy backers over those of their constituents at large. What's more, we have seen that the need to raise huge sums of money whittles down the range of positions that "serious" candidates can take, ultimately ensuring that both Democratic and Republican candidates will have very similar stances on important economic and fiscal issues before any votes are actually cast. So, while the Supreme Court has consistently ruled that campaign contributions should be considered a form of protected free speech, an important human right, we have also seen that a system of largely unrestrained finance can undermine democracy. Here again we have a situation in which rights are seen to be at odds with one another, and when the rights of the powerful few seem to prevail against the rights of the many. But as sociologists we should point out that it does not need to be like this. There are possible ways in which the right to speech and the right to participation in democracy could be better balanced in U.S. society.

Striking a Balance Between Political Rights in U.S. Society

The Supreme Court decision in 2010 on *Citizens United vs. the FEC* was largely consistent with a number of other previous rulings, in which money spent to influence political elections was considered a form of protected free speech. The Supreme Court did break new ground in this ruling, however, by giving corporations and unions this right as well, as long as the money is given to so called "independent" organizations campaigning on a candidate's behalf, but not placed in the candidate's campaign coffers directly. The Supreme Court interpretation of campaign money as speech set some very significant constraints on what might be done to promote democratic rights in the United States. However, the composition of the Supreme Court does change, and so one long-term strategy might be work to influence that composition in hopes that future courts will be more willing to change course and allow more significant limits on campaign expenditures.

Rather than waiting for the court to change, some activists and elected officials are enacting another long-term strategy by building support for a constitutional amendment that would give Congress the power to more thoroughly limit the amount of money individuals can spend on politics. Indeed, more than one proposal for such an amendment has already been introduced to Congress (see Box 3.1 below for one example). While amending the U.S. Constitution is a daunting undertaking—requiring both a two-thirds majority in both the House and the Senate and ratification by three quarters of the states in order to succeed—it is nonetheless possible. Advocates of prohibition were, after all, able to achieve this goal for what proved to be a much less worthy cause in the Eighteenth Amendment. Consequently, backers of a new amendment to allow Congress to more stringently limit campaign contributions have been working to build support around the country. As of 2013, 16 states and many other cities have passed resolutions supporting such an amendment (Nichols 2013).

Others advocate publically financed elections as a means to promote increased democracy rights in the United States. Lessig (2011), for instance, envisions an election finance system in which every American is given a certain amount of money—say $200—in "democracy vouchers" out of their federal taxes they pay on income, payroll, or purchases of gasoline or cigarettes. Individuals can then divvy up their vouchers however they like to candidates of their choice. The catch is that any candidate that accepts these vouchers must forgo other private campaign contributions beyond a certain level, say another $200 per person. This system isn't at odds with the Supreme Court's interpretation of campaign money as speech, because it allows candidates to choose whether or not they will participate. Rather, the system here understands that the political "speech" of Americans without large sums of money to give is at a significant disadvantage compared to the speech of the very wealthy, who amplify their ideas and arguments with lots of dollar signs. This policy reform hopes to make other voices louder by backing them with public funds.

> **Box 3.1 The "Democracy is for People" Proposed Constitutional Amendment**
>
> *Section I*
>
> Whereas the right to vote in public elections belongs only to natural persons as citizens of the United States, so shall the ability to make contributions and expenditures to influence the outcomes of public elections belong only to natural persons in accordance with this Article.
>
> *Section II*
>
> Nothing in this Constitution shall be construed to restrict the power of Congress and the States to protect the integrity and fairness of the electoral process, limit the corrupting influence of private wealth in public elections, and guarantee the dependence of elected officials on the people alone by taking actions which may include the establishment of systems of public financing for elections ...
>
> *Section III*
>
> Nothing in this Article shall be construed to alter the freedom of the press.
>
> *Source*: "Democracy is for People Amendment" introduced in the 2013 Congress by Senator Bernie Sanders and Congressman Ted Deutch (http://teddeutch.house.gov/uploadedfiles/amendment_fact_sheet.pdf)

This chapter underscores the more general point that, while in abstract, human rights are about what is just and fair, in the real world rights have much to do with power and interpretation. U.S. society is premised upon both the right to free speech and the right to democratic participation, but we have seen here that—just as with the rights to property and wellbeing covered in the last chapter—the rights of some have been interpreted in such a way that they undermine the rights of the majority, in this case the right to have the opportunity to influence elections and be represented by officials primarily legislating out of concern for the wellbeing of his or her constituents. A better balance could be struck between these rights, but this will not happen on its own accord. If it happens at all, it will only be through the development of a national grassroots campaign powerful enough to make rights to both free speech and democracy real in America.

DISCUSSION QUESTIONS

1. The Center for Responsive Politics, a non-profit public interest organization, runs an important website that allows users to learn who the main financial contributors are to congressional and presidential candidates. Go to the website at

www.opensecrets.org/races/index.php to look up a senator or house member from your state. What can you find? How do you think the contributors listed here relate to this member's of Congress position and voting record on important issues?

2. What is the difference between personal and institutional corruption? Do you agree with Lessig that institutional corruption is a greater threat to contemporary American democracy than personal corruption? Why or why not?

3. The concluding section discussed several reform ideas to balance rights between speech and democratic participation. Do any of these ideas capture your imagination? Do any of these reforms seem like they might be effective, or perhaps hopelessly naïve? Please explain your thinking.

IV: Racism and the Human Right to be Treated Equally Before the Law

Two Florida legal cases drew comparisons with one another in 2013. In the first case, Marissa Alexander—an African American woman—was sentenced to 20 years in prison for firing a gun in the air to protect herself from what she feared would be a physical attack from her husband (Lee 2012). Alexander thought she was well within her rights to do so. Her husband had been previously arrested for an attack that had put her in the hospital when she was pregnant, and Florida has a "stand your ground law," which gives citizens the authority to use deadly force when they believe their life is threatened or if they fear they might suffer severe bodily harm. However, the judge overseeing Alexander's case refused to allow her to invoke the law, claiming that she might have been able to leave through the front or back door to escape harm (Lee 2012). As a result, Alexander was found guilty of assault with a deadly weapon and taken away from her two small children to be locked up behind bars.

The Alexander case was compared to another court battle you have likely heard about: On the night of February 26, 2012, neighborhood watch volunteer George Zimmerman followed sixteen-year-old Trayvon Martin as he walked through the gated community in which both individuals lived. Zimmerman alleges that Martin looked suspicious because of the hooded sweatshirt he wore, but the case has attracted immense scrutiny around the United States because many people also believe that Zimmerman thought Martin looked suspicious because he was a young African American male. Zimmerman called the police, saying "these fucking punks, they always get away." The police dispatcher instructed Zimmerman to stay in his car and stop pursuing Martin. But Zimmerman didn't comply. Instead he got out of his car and, while the exact details of what happened in the resulting altercation are not clear, ultimately George Zimmerman shot Trayvon Martin dead. Despite the fact that Martin had no weapon, but was only found with a bag of Skittles and a bottle of iced tea, Zimmerman invoked self-defense when he was put on trial for the killing. But as we all know, the results were much different in this case compared to that of Alexander's. Zimmerman was deemed innocent. These two cases, when compared side by side, are unsettling. They indicate that not everyone is treated equally before the law in U.S. society.

The Universal Declaration of Human Rights insists that no person should be discriminated against based on race, and that governments should treat all people equally. When the document was adopted by the member nations of the UN in 1948, the political organization of much of the world was openly racist. Many of the signatory nations themselves maintained policies that intentionally promoted racial inequality, both within and between the societies they governed. But **social movements** were already well underway in Asia, Africa, the Caribbean, and the United States that were demanding racial equality. Many of these movements achieved real and lasting success. In the formerly colonized regions, these movements helped rid their nations of domination by external powers. And within the former colonial powers themselves, movements made important headway toward racial equality. Of course, rights were not granted by the powerful because it was the fair and appropriate thing to do, but because these movements demanded and required it.

U.S. society in 1948, in which the powerful Civil Rights movement was about to emerge, is an important example. By pioneering new grassroots tactics and expertly wielding more time-tested protest methods—such as boycotts, sit-ins, marches, community-wide protests, and voter registration drives—black leaders would force white power-holders to acknowledge the fundamental human rights of all people regardless of race (McAdam 1983). The successes in the 1950s and 1960s were real, as were those of the Chicano and the Red Power movements that followed. In particular, the Civil Rights movement was successful at achieving increased civil and political rights of African Americans by, for instance, abolishing **Jim Crow segregation**—maintained through legal policies that intentionally discriminate based on race—and by securing the right to vote *in practice*, not just as something that is technically guaranteed as a right in the Fifteenth Amendment to the U.S. Constitution. Many in the Civil Rights movement did not want to stop with these victories, but hoped to advance broader wellbeing rights for people of color who had been, as a whole, excluded for generations from the better-paying jobs in America's economy. The existing social structure that upheld whites over other racial groups, however, proved to be too resistant to much more change, and so the movement fell short in this regard. For this reason, even with a black president currently in office, racism remains an enduring characteristic of U.S. society.

In this chapter, we will consider what sociologists mean when they talk about **race** and **racism**, paying particular attention to the ways that differences between races are reproduced over generations even in a society that often claims to be "colorblind." In doing so, we will use the differential enforcement of U.S. criminal justice policies regarding illegal drugs in order to explore violations of human rights in relation to race throughout our society. Finally, we will consider what particular remedies citizens are pursuing in order to achieve greater racial justice in the United States.

Human Rights, Race, and the U.S. "War on Drugs"

Justin Laboy says he had fallen head over heels for the new girl who sat next to him in class at a high school in Palm Beach County, Florida. So much so, in fact, that he asked her to be his date for the upcoming senior prom. The new student turned him down, but when she asked Justin if he knew how to get some weed, he still had his hopes up. He told her that he could get some for her, even though he personally never smoked. Justin tracked down a bag of marijuana from a friend of his cousin, and when he gave it to his heartthrob, she insisted on paying $25 for it. Justin reluctantly accepted the money, and upon the completion of this transaction, he had been ensnared in a drug bust that would cost him dearly. The woman he was so attracted to wasn't really a high school student at all, she was a recent graduate from the police academy doing undercover work. She was just playing the role of "student," with a fake Facebook account and all (Brown 2012).

We can choose to believe Justin or not regarding the particular details of his story, for instance if he really did not smoke weed himself as he claims, and whether or not he was a petty drug dealer at his high school.[1] But what we do know for certain is that Justin was an honor roll student with no previous criminal record. We also know that he had to spend a week in jail when he was arrested after the drug sting. And when confronted with the undercover officer's testimony against him about the drug deal, he pled guilty to a felony charge. The plea deal included no further jail time, but the felony on his record means Justin will never be able to pursue his dream of joining the Air Force. Perhaps most significantly, it means Justin will be placed at a tremendous disadvantage on the job market, as he will be asked about his criminal record in future job applications and will be competing against other qualified candidates without a felony conviction. Finally, Florida, like several other U.S. states, sharply curtails the voting rights of felons. As a result of this high school indiscretion, Justin may never be able to vote in any of the important elections that will take place over the course of his life.

Justin's story, like the 97 other students caught up in this particular drug sting at his former high school in Palm Beach, along with millions of other Americans, is one of a life irrevocably impacted by the "war on drugs." But this "war" has not been waged equally throughout American society. People of color, like Justin, are disproportionately its targets. This point becomes very clear when we compare Justin's story to the stories of self-professed drug dealers on a private college campus that were studied by Rafik Mohamed and Erik Fritsvold (2011). While many drug dealers might take elaborate precautions to avoid being busted, these white dealers, who were mostly from wealthy families, took few precautions to avoid being busted. Indeed, Mohamed and Fritsvold found that there was practically no reason for them to be concerned, as they largely escaped the attention of the police and were mostly ignored by college administrators who did not want to upset parents or draw negative attention to their campuses. Though these students were distributing weed and various prescription medicines for illicit purposes, they mostly did not think of themselves as criminals, and that's pretty much how their community thought of them too. In one telling story, after one of these white and well-to-do dealers was robbed of his money and drugs, he felt entitled to report it to the police. And when the police caught the suspect, they actually returned the stolen money (though they of course did not hand over the stolen drugs, which the dealer wisely did not claim as his own).

These examples illustrate that while race is a social construction, having no biological basis, it is a definition of the world that has real consequences in the lives of Americans. On the one hand, racism results in systematic disadvantages for those born as people of color. But the other side of racism, **white privilege**, results in comparative advantages in the lives of others. Peggy McIntosh has defined white privilege as an "invisible knapsack containing a set of unearned privileges." Robert Jensen (1998) argues that this privilege is unearned and does not necessarily need to be sought after. Rather, it is a privilege that simply accrues to white people, as a whole, when living in a racist society. The dorm-room dealers in Mohamed and Fritsvold's study were obviously beneficiaries of white privilege. But so too are white drug users as a whole.

Research has consistently demonstrated that white people and people of color use illegal drugs at very similar rates (SMAHS 2012). Those convicted of drug crimes in the United States, however, are overwhelmingly people of color. While non-Hispanic whites make up almost 63 percent of the U.S. population, they make up only 30 percent of those individuals serving time in state prisons for drug sales or possession (Carson and Sabol 2012). Blacks, on the other hand, make up about 13 percent of the U.S. population. But this group comprise a full 50 percent of those persons in state prisons for drug crimes. Clearly then, there is a tremendous underrepresentation of white drug users and sellers in the prison system, and an overrepresentation of people of color. But how did this disparity come about?

For one, it came about because of drug policies that have historically targeted people of color. Drugs have not always been criminalized in the United States, and the process by which they became illegal has strong racial overtones. For instance, during the early 1900s, anti-drug campaigners played upon racist images and antipathy toward Chinese immigrants in efforts to criminalize opium (Provine 2011). Likewise, during the same period, hyped-up stories of out-of-control black people high on cocaine were used to successfully make that drug illegal. And in the 1910s and 1920s, racial sentiment against Mexicans and Mexican Americans was mobilized in efforts to criminalize marijuana (Provine 2011).

Racial biases continue to be embedded in drug laws today. In her book *The New Jim Crow: Mass Incarceration in the Age of Colorblindness*, legal scholar Michele Alexander (2012) writes that while crack cocaine and powdered cocaine are pharmacologically almost identical, crack cocaine—which is a more affordable form of cocaine available to poor people in inner cities—was demonized in the 1980s and a federal law, the *Anti Drug Abuse Act* of 1986, was passed that was so punitive it mandated a 5-year sentence for possession of 5 grams. This new sentence was exceedingly lopsided compared to the sentence for the more expensive powdered cocaine favored by many wealthy whites, at which 500 grams (or a ratio of 100 to 1) would be required to trigger a mandatory 5-year sentence (Alexander 2012). While Congress moved in 2010 to raise the amount of crack needed to mandate the 5-year sentence to 28 grams, a huge disparity between sentencing for possession of the two types of cocaine remains today, which has ulti-mately impacted the racial composition of America's prison population (Abrams 2010).

The difference in how people and communities are policed—based upon race and wealth—is another factor that produces the huge racial disparities in drug convictions in America, as the contrasting experiences of Justin Lebloy and the campus "dorm-room dealers" indicate. One telling statistic, uncovered by an **American Civil Liberties Union** investigation, is that while whites and blacks use marijuana at similar rates, African Americans are 3.7 times more likely to be arrested for the drug. Some of this has to do with **personal racism** on the part of police officers. Most of us are born into a racist culture in the United States, which typically ignores the ways that racism has benefited white people over the generations. This culture also typically blames people of color for not achieving full economic equality with whites, and often portrays people of color—especially young men—as suspects and as being potentially dangerous. To use one easy-to-imagine exam-ple, a police officer, consciously or unconsciously, is acting on the prejudices of our broader society when he or she never looks twice at a white drug user after giving her a speeding ticket, but instead lets her go on her merry way. Likewise, this same police officer is acting on broader cultural prejudices when subjecting a Latino driver and his car to a thorough search after pulling him over for the same traffic violation. The police officer might justify this different treatment by saying the Latino driver "looked suspicious," but we should remember that we live in a society that has trained him or her to think that way, while also allowing many white drug users to evade apprehension.

Of course, communities are also policed very differently, which has to do with **institutional racism**, or the ways that economic processes and governmental policies privilege and disadvantage different groups based on race. When thinking about insti-tutional racism, we need to keep a couple of things in mind. First, we need to remem-ber that the U.S. government maintained official policies of racial domination for centuries by usurping Native American land through conquest and by forcing indig-enous Americans onto reservations, by upholding slavery, and then endorsing policies of Jim Crow segregation. The U.S. government also made racism official policy by confiscating land jointly owned by Mexicans in the American Southwest, and then discriminating against this group in their ancestral home. Considering all the cumula-tive impacts of this racist history, when the U.S. government eliminated overtly racist laws in the wake of the social movements of the 1960s and 1970s, it didn't bring about racial equality. Rather, this history of overt racism remained embedded in America's contemporary economy and social fabric. As Figure 4.1 indicates, white people are much less likely to live in poverty compared to other groups, with about 11.6 percent of whites living below the official poverty threshold. On the other hand, the poverty rate is more than double that for American Indians and Alaska Natives, Latinos, and African Americans (Macartney, Bishaw, and Fontenot 2013). Differences in wealth are even more staggering. On average, white people hold six times the wealth compared to that owned by African Americans and Latinos (Lowery 2013).

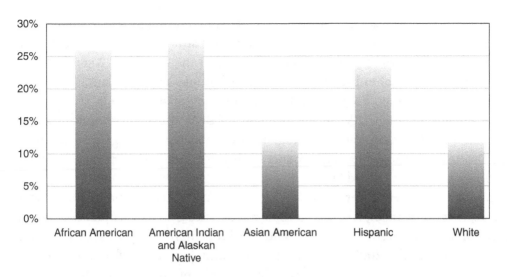

Figure 4.1 Poverty Rates by Race (2011)

Source: Macartney, Bishaw, and Fontenot (2013) "Poverty Rates for Selected Detailed Race and Hispanic Groups by State and Place: 2007–2011."

Racism has been embedded in our economy, and this is reflected in the social and racial geography and urban development of virtually all American cities. In many metropolitan areas segregation by race is as great or greater than it was during the period of the **Civil Rights Movement** of the 1950s and 1960s. Needless to say, police departments treat wealthier neighborhoods predominated by white people very differently compared to poorer neighborhoods with greater numbers of people of color. Some cities, in fact, have implemented official policies to aggressively police poorer neighborhoods and subject residents there to routine searches, which in itself results in a violation of both the human right to privacy and the right to be free from racial discrimination. New York City's recently overturned "stop and frisk" policy is perhaps the most notorious example. In 2012, for example, the New York City police stopped 473,644 innocent people and frisked, or searched, half of them (NYCLU 2013). Not everyone is equally subjected to these policies. While whites make up about 45 percent of all New Yorkers, they accounted for only 10 percent of the stops. And frisks were much more likely to be carried out in black and Latino neighborhoods compared to whiter sections of the city. Perhaps most telling, while young Latino and black men, between the ages of 14 and 24, make up only 4.7 percent of the total population of the city, they were the group that made up more than 40 percent of all police stops (NYCLU 2013).

Clearly then, if members of various racial groups in America do drugs at similar rates, these kinds of racialized policing strategies, in which people of color are stopped and searched more, helps explain the discrepancies by race for those in U.S. prisons for drug crimes. And we should remember that similar dynamics are at work at all levels of the criminal justice system, from trials, to sentencing, to decisions about probation and early release. By following these dynamics, we can begin to understand why almost 9 percent of black men and 4 percent of Latino men in their late 20s are in prison today, compared to 1.5 percent of whites of the same age (Wagner 2012). While not all crimes committed by different racial groups are equivalent, as they are with drug use, we should keep in mind that almost half of all people in U.S. prisons today are there for drugs (Alexander 2012). We should also keep in mind that the racial biases in the enforcement of drugs laws exist in the policing of all kinds of crimes, which taken together help produce such profoundly different rates of incarceration by race in the United States.

Thinking about these differential rates of incarceration, and the processes we have discussed that create them, reveals that the United States is a racist nation, even if it is mostly populated by individuals who would, if asked, emphatically insist that they are not racist (Bonilla-Silva 2009). Typically, people working in America's criminal justice system believe in equality between persons in principle, but they nonetheless subconsciously act on their socialization in our racist culture that teaches that some people are more "suspect" than others. Politicians and law enforcement officials also enact policies, like New York's "stop and frisk," that disproportionately impact communities of color, even if such policies seem to be colorblind on their surface.

This is one example of the ways race functions in the United States. We would find a similar story if we were to examine America's educational system, or if we were to examine the hiring and promotion practices of large corporations. But we examined instead the United State's "war on drugs" and found that it unfairly impacts people of color in the nation. Its consequences are devastating, locking convicts away from their families for years and even decades, revoking their right to vote—permanently in some states—and dramatically diminishing their employment prospects throughout their entire life. Because the impact is so severe, and because the implementation is so uneven, the U.S. "war on drugs" has resulted in the widespread violation of the human rights of Americans. The next section considers what might be done in order to promote greater racial justice.

Promoting Racial Justice in the United States

An important beginning place to achieve greater racial justice in the United States would be for whites to become more open to discussions of racism in order to increase their awareness of the ways that they have been privileged by the United States's history of overt, or what is known as state-sanctioned, racism and the continuation of "**colorblind racism**" today. Of course, as hip-hop radio host and popular video blogger Jay Smooth (2011) notes, this can be very difficult because we are in a society that thinks about racism in an either/or kind of way. Typically, we think that someone is either a racist or not a racist, implying that he or she is either a good or a bad person. If we compared this to health procedures, Smooth says that this is the "tonsils" model of thinking about race: "What me? I can't have said anything racist because I had my prejudice removed last year." Rather than thinking about racism as an either/or phenomena, Smooth argues we should understand that we have been raised in a culture and taught—consciously or unconsciously—to make racist assumptions. In this regard, because we can't remove ourselves from our culture, we should think about and deal with race, not like tonsils that we remove once and then forget about, but much more regularly, like brushing our teeth, something we should do everyday[2] (Smooth 2011).

We should also recognize that racism is deeply embedded in American society, so it will take concerted political action to secure the full array of rights in this society for all people. Indeed, political advocacy for racial equality has been ongoing both before and after the powerful social movements of the 1960s and 1970s. Most recently, the North Carolina chapter of the **NAACP** led large "Moral Monday" protests in 2013 at the state capital, drawing thousands of people and sometimes involving large **civil disobedience** protests, in which hundreds have been arrested, in order to promote racial justice and other human rights in the state (Wing 2013). Also in 2013, the verdict of the Trayvon Martin case discussed earlier in the chapter sparked ongoing protests and dialogue across the nation about racial profiling. History teaches that social movements can have a real impact in terms of securing human rights, but the movements today need more adherents in order to achieve greater racial justice in our society.

There are a number of specific goals activists might pursue in order to diminish the racist impacts of the "war on drugs," such as pushing city-wide policies that would prevent police departments from discriminating based on race, as recently happened in New York City after enough people became outraged over "stop and frisk." Michele Alexander also encourages activists to work to eliminate the **mandatory minimum** drug sentences that uniformly impose long sentences on those convicted of drug crimes, regardless of the individual circumstances of the person accused. We might also work to end the widespread practice that denies felons, including those convicted for the possession of drugs, of their right to vote while in prison, probation, or for life.

Paul Butler, a law professor who was formerly a federal prosecutor who worked to send drug dealers and drug users behind bars, advocates an even more far-reaching goal. As a prosecutor, Butler (2009) became convinced that the drug war was ultimately unwinnable and that it unfairly impacted people of color. He now advocates the decriminalization of drugs. Such an approach does not mean we need to ignore the fact that drug use can do real harm to people and their communities. But the approach instead insists that criminalizing drugs has not diminished this harm, but has instead increased it. After all, alcohol can play a destructive role in some people's lives too, but we can see from the history of prohibition in the 1920s that its criminalization was hardly a recipe to reduce the harm that alcohol caused to the American social fabric. The **harm reduction approach** advocated by Butler would decriminalize drugs, but would also work to create public awareness campaigns about the potential negative consequences of drug use and would allocate more resources to the treatment of addiction. The approach would further seek to create a context—by for instance monitoring the ingredients in drugs and providing needle exchanges—that would make drug use safer for those who continue to use them.

Regardless of the specific policy changes we might pursue, by for instance working to make drug sentencing less severe or working to abolish the "war on drugs" altogether, Alexander (2012) encourages us not to do this using a "colorblind" framework. When doing so, we should remember that the whole premise of the drug war is one that thinks millions of people of color are expendable, and that the harm done to their families and communities is justified. It is based on a whole way of seeing the world that ignores large-scale suffering caused by the mass depravation of fundamental human rights. Instead, Alexander argues, such efforts should be bound up in a broad movement committed to transform America in order to achieve human rights for all.

DISCUSSION QUESTIONS

1. It was noted earlier in this section that many American metropolitan areas remain as segregated today as they were decades ago. Is your own community segregated? Can you think of different neighborhoods that are predominated by certain racial groups, including those predominated by whites? If so, how do you think life is different in these various communities?

2. Given that whites and members of other racial groups use drugs at similar rates, what are the major reasons for the disparity between those in U.S. prisons convicted of drug crimes?

3. Can you think of some other examples of "colorblind" institutional racism, or the social/economic dynamics that create racial differences despite being race neutral on the surface?

4. Look again at the Universal Declaration of Human Rights. Which human rights are violated or put at risk by the particular way the "war on drugs" has been prosecuted in America?

5. What do you think about Butler's (2009) advocacy of a "harm reduction program," rather than the criminalization of drugs? What do you think might be the benefits and drawbacks of such a policy change in the United States?

Notes

1 You can listen to Justin tell his story by going to http://www.thisamericanlife.org/radio-archives/episode/457/what-i-did-for-love?act=2.
2 You can watch Smooth's talk by going to: http://www.youtube.com/watch?v=MbdxeFcQtaU.

V: Sexism and the Right to Bodily Integrity

～～✕～～

In 2013, a group of 13 students at the University of Southern California filed a complaint with the federal Department of Education, alleging discrimination because their university failed to take reports of their rapes seriously, and by so doing failed to maintain a safe environment for them and other women on campus (Kingkade 2013). These women shared painful stories in their complaint. One woman wrote that a college administrator decided to dismiss charges against her ex-boyfriend, who had admitted raping her, because he wanted to create an "educative" process, rather than one that was punitive. Another student wrote that campus police decided not to classify her **sexual assault** as **rape**—contrary to the official definition of rape in the United States—because the perpetrator stopped before having an orgasm. Another woman stated that, after she informed campus police officials that she was raped at a fraternity party, she was given a lecture that she should expect such consequences if she goes out to parties and gets drunk. Other women wrote in the complaint that even after their assailants were deemed guilty of having committed a rape by school administrators, they were given light punishments and in many cases allowed to stay on campus through graduation (Kingkade 2013).

These incidents offer several reminders, first that rape and sexual assault are all too common in the United States, even at places like college campuses that seem—on the surface—to be safe and welcoming to all. Second, these stories remind us that far too many of those who commit rapes and other acts of violence against women go unpunished. Importantly, this story is also a reminder that women refuse to tolerate such abuse and assault, but are organizing against it and are otherwise working to assert their human rights. The federal complaint against the University of Southern California is, in fact, just one of an unprecedented number of student complaints made to the Department of Education against colleges and universities—including Swarthmore, Occidental, Dartmouth, the University of North Carolina, and the University of Colorado—for not taking rape seriously and therefore failing to create a non-discriminatory environment for women (Kingkade 2013).

In this chapter, we will consider the extent of rape in U.S. society as a pressing human rights concern. When doing so, we will place rape and violence against women within a larger context of gender inequality in the United States, making the argument that we live in a sexist, or patriarchal society. Finally, we will consider what women and men are doing in order to promote and achieve women's rights, as basic human rights, across the country.

Rape and the Violation of the Right to Bodily Integrity in U.S. Society

The Universal Declaration of Human Rights proclaims that all people have a right to security and a right not to suffer from "cruel, inhuman or degrading treatment." Rape certainly constitutes a violation of these rights. And to be sure, the impact of rape does not only happen during the moment of the crime and its immediate aftermath. On the contrary, rape survivors are more likely to report experiencing frequent headaches, difficulty sleeping, and poorer mental and physical health compared to others who were not made to experience this kind of violence (Black et al. 2011). But what exactly is rape?

The FBI's "uniform crime reporting" program defines rape this way:

> Penetration, no matter how slight, of the vagina or anus with any body part or object, or oral penetration by a sex organ of another person, without the consent of the victim.

This definition is very important, because a common **rape myth** holds otherwise, that in order to constitute rape, it must be accompanied by violence or the threat of violence. However, the legal definition of rape in the United States means that a person has committed the crime by penetrating another person's body without consent, including instances in which she or he is unable to do so because of being too drunk, high, or having been drugged.

Rape and sexual assault, unfortunately, are common experiences in the United States. Survey research reveals that 1.3 million women experience rape or attempted rape every year, and that 18 percent of women—almost one in five—will experience rape or attempted rape sometime in their lifetimes[1] (Black et al. 2011). But of course, these are only estimates. We are uncertain about exactly how many rapes occur each year because they so often go unreported. One study of college women found that only 11 percent of rape survivors reported their victimization to authorities (Wolitzky-Taylor et al. 2011).

There are a number of reasons why only a small portion of rapes committed in the United States are reported. For one, and contrary to another rape myth that holds that rapes are typically committed by strangers in outdoor places, rapes are most often committed by husbands, boyfriends, dates, friends, and other acquaintances. According to one large survey, more than half of all rapes were committed by an intimate partner, while another 40 percent of rapes were committed by an acquaintance (Black et al. 2011). This means that women might not report rapes sometimes out of a concern of upending their family and social life. While hospitals, universities, and local anti-sexual assault groups often provide crucial support to rape survivors, sometimes this is not enough. Despite this support, women may choose not to report rapes due to worries that authorities will not take accusations seriously and, even worse, will revictimize a survivor by putting her on trail, for instance by subjecting her style of clothing, her past dating, and her partying habits to close scrutiny. Finally, another important reason why women might not report sexual assault is that rapists commonly use alcohol and drugs as a weapon to sedate their victims. Having been rendered unconscious, a rape victim might have uncertainties about the nature of the crime and even the identity of the perpetrator.

So rapes go unreported for understandable reasons. But the tragic consequence is that many rapists go unpunished and are allowed to remain free to victimize others. Another consequence is that women who do not report rapes are less likely to secure the medical and psychological care necessary to heal (Wolitzky-Taylor et al. 2011). In the next section, we will attempt to understand why rape is so widespread in the United States.

Rape in Social Context

Former Army Sergeant Rebekah Havrilla gave courageous testimony in front of the U.S. Senate on March 12, 2013, in which she described her assault by another Army officer in Afghanistan and the failure of the U.S. military to prosecute and remove the rapist from its ranks (Saenz 2013). Havrilla told Senators that after she first reported her assault, military officials declined to investigate. During this period, she and the man who assaulted her remained at the same base, and upon encountering him again she was further traumatized. Months after the rape, she was told by a friend that the perpetrator had posted pictures of her assault on a pornographic website. Havrilla reported the assault once again to military officials, who now decided to conduct an investigation. After a male military police officer questioned Havrilla for four hours, forcing her to look over the internet pictures of her rape, higher ranking officials decided not to pursue a court martial or any other disciplinary action against the assailant (Saenz 2013). Unfortunately, Havrilla's experiences are not uncommon in the U.S. military, which conducted a survey in 2013 that estimated that 26,000 service members were raped or sexually assaulted the preceding year. Only a small number, 3,378—or about 13 percent—were reported, and of these only 190 cases were sent to court martial proceedings (Goodman and Moynihan 2013).

Thinking about the high incidence of sexual assault in the military makes clear that not every woman is equally at risk. Social context matters a great deal. For one thing, women in social institutions that are dominated by men are at greater risk of being victimized by rape and other sexual assault. The U.S. military certainly counts as a male-dominated organization. While the numbers of women service members is growing, women still account for a small percentage of the total number of soldiers and an even smaller number of top officers in the Army, Navy, Air Force, and Marines. As U.S. policy now stands, when a woman is sexually assaulted, she is supposed to report the crime to her commanding officer. This is problematic for many women, however, because the commanding officer may be a friend of the perpetrator, or he may be the perpetrator himself. And because the commanding officer is very likely to be a man, he might be more willing to give another man accused of committing a sexual assault the benefit of the doubt. Furthermore, he might be less willing to enact a punishment that would harm the accused assailant's career. What's more, even if a reported rape is investigated and it goes to military court, a guilty verdict could still be reversed by a commanding general, also very likely to be a man, as recently happened in one prominent Air Force case when a general overturned a jury's conviction of officer James Wilkerson for aggravated sexual assault. In so doing, the general re-enlisted the offender into the service at full rank (Billeaud 2013). In this kind of male-dominated institution, rapists are more likely to go unpunished, and so can continue to commit grave violations of human rights.

The U.S. military is an important example of a male-dominated institution in which women are at increased risk of experiencing rape and sexual assault. Some of the unique characteristics of the military might exacerbate the risks women face, but we should also ask, is the military entirely exceptional? Think, for instance, about your college or university. Are both men and women equally represented amongst the high-ranking administrators? If not, and if women have been historically underrepresented in top decision-making positions as they have been at most schools, do you think this is a factor influencing whether or not the school prioritizes the rights of women and aggressively investigates and punishes sexual assault? Also, please think about what the party scene is like. Is it one in which women and men hold an equal share of power, or is it one in which women have less control? Universities, for instance, often threaten to give harsh punishments for those caught drinking alcohol in dorms, and this can have the unintended consequence of pushing female underclassmen to fraternity parties—which sometimes feature sexist themes such as "bros and hos," "CEO and secretary hos," or "Victoria's Secret" (Armstrong, Hamilton, and Sweeney 2006). Of course, male fraternity members control access to alcohol at these parties, and some may choose to use it as a weapon in order to inebriate women beyond consciousness. Underclass women may be further disadvantaged in these situations if they lack transportation to and from fraternity parties, instead relying on frat members to supply rides (Armstrong, Hamilton, and Sweeney 2006). Such an unequal context between men and women is conducive to rape and sexual assault, and helps explain why rates of rape and sexual assault are higher at universities compared to the U.S. population as a whole. In fact, an estimated one fifth to one quarter of female students will experience a sexual assault before graduating from college (Krebs et al. 2009).

Thinking about how male domination increases risks posed to women from sexual assault in the military or at college helps us understand how this dynamic plays out in our larger society as well. Why is it that this violation of fundamental human rights is so prevalent in the United States? Ultimately, the answer is because we live in a "**patriarchal**," or sexist society, in which women hold relatively less power compared to men, and in which the activities historically associated with men are valued more highly than those activities historically associated with women. We can mobilize evidence from a number of different areas in order to make this case.

First, we can look at economic data. Women's annual income on average is about 75 percent of that of the average male worker (DeNavas-Walt, Proctor, and Smith 2012). Some of this discrepancy has to do with workplace discrimination, in which male employees are more likely to garner higher wages and promotions compared to women, regardless of education levels. And some of this difference is due to gender socialization in the United States that channels women and men into different occupations. Those occupations that have been historically filled by women, the so-called "**pink-collar jobs**," are typically less well paid compared to male-dominated activities, regardless of educational requirements, skill level, and importance. For instance, according to the U.S. Bureau of Labor Statistics, the average carpenter made $44,000 a year in 2012 and the average carpet installer made $41,000. These two occupations that are predominated by men are paid much more highly compared to the average preschool teacher, who made just $33,000 a year. While building houses, laying carpets, and keeping four-year olds happy, mentally active, and safe all require skill and are all important to our society, these jobs are not all equally valued or remunerated, which has to do with the history of **sexism** in America.

In addition to these factors, women earn less as a whole compared to men because women are more likely to take time away from work in order to care for children, either opting to spend less time at work on a daily or weekly basis or leaving the workplace altogether for a number of years while children are young. While it might at first seem like there is an element of "choice" here, we should remember that children can be raised either by mothers, by fathers, or by both mothers and fathers equally. But in a sexist society, this is work that is disproportionately allocated to women. And while raising children may be immensely enriching to a person's life and crucial for our society, it also is given practically no economic value and, quite the contrary, is an activity that can exact a real penalty in terms of women's earning potentials over the course of their lives.

Beyond looking at economic data, we can also look to politics and the law for evidence that we live in a sexist society. Historically, of course, women enjoyed very few legal rights in the United States. The right to vote, secured through the 14th Amendment to the U.S. Constitution, was only achieved in 1919 after women had mounted a powerful, widespread, and decades-long social movement. During that era, women had few rights regarding self-determination compared to men, and were often instead considered the legal property of husbands and fathers. What's more, it wasn't until the 1960s and 1970s, due to the achievements of the **Second Wave** of the Women's Movement, that it became illegal for a husband to rape his wife.

Today, the male-dominated nature of U.S. society continues to be reflected in its legal code, most crucially in the failure to ratify the proposed Equal Rights Amendment and the international Convention on the Elimination of All Forms of Discrimination against Women. The Equal Rights Amendment (ERA) was drafted by Alice Paul, who was a key leader of the movement to secure women's right to the vote. The proposed amendment to the Constitution simply states: "Equality of rights under the law shall not be denied or abridged by the United States or by any state on account of sex." The ERA languished for decades until it was championed and pushed forward by the Second Wave of the Women's Movement in the early 1970s. While the amendment secured the supermajority approval needed to pass through Congress, conservative forces mobilized to frame the amendment as a threat to traditional American family values. In the end, 35 states ratified the statement, falling just short of the 38-state total needed to amend the Constitution.

As with the Equal Rights Amendment, U.S. lawmakers have also failed to ratify the international Convention on the Elimination of Discrimination Against Women (CEDAW). President Jimmy Carter signed the treaty in 1980, but in order to become part of the law of the land, it must be approved by two thirds of the Senate. So far, this has proved insurmountable for women's rights advocates who urge the adoption of CEDAW. Consequently, the United States is among only a tiny handful of nations in the world that have not ratified the accord, including Iran, Somalia, and Sudan. Of course, it would be a terrible mistake to conclude that gender inequality is worse in the United States because it has not joined the Convention compared to other nations, like Afghanistan or Pakistan, that have. This is far from the case. Many international human rights treaties, like CEDAW, have weak enforcement mechanisms and offer only few legal avenues to challenge the male domination that has been embedded in social institutions for generations. Even so, ratification is at the very least symbolically important because it is a way national governments communicate to the world, and to their own citizens, the extent to which women's basic human rights are acknowledged. The failure of U.S. lawmakers to ratify CEDAW is further evidence that we live in a sexist society.[2]

One important reason why the United States has not ratified CEDAW and the Equal Rights Amendment—along with other important laws that could promote pay equity and provide more support for families with children—is that U.S. political institutions remain largely the province of men. While women made record gains in the U.S. Senate in 2012, for instance, they now make up only 20 percent of all Senators. The situation in the U.S. House is even worse, where women make up only 18 percent of all Representatives. On a state level, women remain underrepresented, filling a little less than 25 percent of legislative seats (CAWP 2013).

We don't only need to look at economic and legal/political evidence to understand that the United States remains a sexist society; we might come to a similar conclusion simply by turning on the TV, going to popular websites, or opening up a magazine. Women are constantly **objectified** throughout our media. This is a process of dehumanization in which women are not represented as fully developed persons, but as bodies that exist primarily for male sexual pleasure or as desirable ornaments that can enhance male prestige. And it doesn't help matters that the actual bodies being represented are literally impossible to achieve for average, healthy persons. Many of the women featured in our mass media are dangerously thin, have had their bodies altered through surgical processes, and have had normal blemishes, wrinkles, and fat removed digitally on computer screens after the cameras have been turned off. These representations of women have consequences because they quite literally teach us all how to see the world, but from a male-oriented perspective. It encourages men to view women's bodies as things, while compelling women to achieve an impossible ideal of beauty. While men's bodies might well be increasingly objectified in contemporary mass media, such treatment pales in comparison to that of women.

Taken together, the sexism that permeates U.S. society, in the workplace, in our political and legal system, and in our media, is all related to the problem of sexual assault and violence against women. Earning lower wages means that women may be economically dependent upon abusive spouses and boyfriends. And the fact that women are underrepresented in higher-level positions in the workplace means that reports of rapes are more likely to go ignored or unpunished by authorities. The fact that women have been a small minority of lawmakers in the United States has meant that our various levels of government have been slow to address problems related to the prevalence of sexual assault and other violations of women's human rights. And the objectification of women's bodies is bound up with, but also helps recreate, a male-dominant society that teaches young people that women's bodies can be divorced from their persons and that they exist for the benefit of men. Millions of Americans, however, reject the sexism that is found throughout U.S. society, and are working to create a more equitable society that guarantees human rights.

Working to Achieve Women's Rights in the United States

The University of Colorado at Colorado Springs sparked national controversy when some of the "tips" that it gave to female students to avoid being sexually assaulted were publicized. The tips, part of the university's "rape aggression defense" class, suggested that as a last resort women might avoid being raped by vomiting or urinating on an attacker, or telling an "attacker that you have a disease or are menstruating" (Mungin 2013). While the helpfulness of this particular advice is highly debatable, in general, many women's rights advocates argue that universities' efforts to reduce sexual assaults on campus by offering self-defense classes and giving women rape avoidance advice are ultimately ineffective and unfair to women. For one, as we discussed earlier, the great majority of sexual assaults are committed by intimate partners or acquaintances, so it is not exactly clear how learning self-defense tactics might help women escape risk when a perpetrator is a husband, boyfriend, or friend.

To the extent that self defense and rape avoidance tips can work, they only do so for individual women in particular situations. In other words, approaches that emphasize advice and training for some women likely would not reduce *overall* rates of rape on campus because it is an individual "solution" to a social, or collective, problem. Sociology professor Monica Ulrich (2011) addresses this issue by asking her students to think about all the possible initiatives that a community might undertake in order to diminish the dangers of drunk driving. Hardly any students ever say things like "don't drive on weekend evenings or on holidays when drunk drivers are more likely to be out." Students, Ulrich reports, hardly ever say things like "learn defensive driving strategies." But this is exactly what women often hear in regard to reducing the risks of being raped, such as "don't wear clothes that are too revealing, always watch your drink, and learn self defense." Quite the contrary, we as a society seem to recognize that while this "advice" might be fine on an individual basis, if we really want to reduce drunk driving we need to more vigorously enforce the laws that criminalize it and ensure that violators have to pay real consequences when they are caught. We don't seem to have this same understanding when it comes to rape and sexual assault. Perhaps most troubling to many women's rights advocates, programs that emphasize rape-avoidance training and self-defense for women unfairly place the responsibility to avoid assault on individual women. When women follow "advice" to protect themselves from sexual assault, they may suffer a loss of freedom and self-determination not experienced by men. But if they should choose not to follow this "advice," by wearing what they would like to wear and going out to have fun on a weekend evening, women might be blamed for their own victimization.

There are alternatives. One kind of institutional intervention that shows promise and has been introduced at some schools instead focuses upon men. The program mandates that incoming male freshmen hear the stories of rape survivors and learn about the legal definition of rape, including that committed when a victim is incapacitated. Male students must also learn about the criminal penalties for rape and learn bystander intervention tactics (Gidycz, Orchowski, and Berkowitz 2011). The commission of rape and sexual assault, after all, has very little to do with experiencing sexual gratification, but is most typically motivated by a desire to demonstrate dominance over women and perform masculinity. Men, therefore, can play an important role in defusing and altering social situations that provide a context for sexual assault, for instance those in which women are objectified and in which men seek to demonstrate their manhood to one another through sexual conquests.

Of course, **feminist** organizations are active on many campuses and other communities throughout the United States. Once, these organizations were extremely powerful and played an important role in shaping our contemporary universities, for instance by pushing for the creation of women's studies departments, by boosting the creation of women's centers on campus, and, as we have already discussed, by challenging their schools to change policies in regard to sexual assault, to increase penalties for perpetrators, and increase support for victims. As we have already discussed at the beginning of this chapter, these organizations are continuing to do extremely important work advocating for women's rights on campus. With more adherents, they could make an even greater impact.

But in order to address the root of this problem, we need to keep in mind that women's right to their bodily integrity and self-determination is deeply bound up with other violations of women's human rights in a male-dominated society. In order to reduce rape and sexual assault, ultimately male dominance itself will have to be challenged and brought to an end. Obviously, it would help to have more women in power in order to create this monumental change. Other nations have had success by implementing rules, either voluntary or legally mandated, that require political parties to run a substantial number of female candidates for office. Many political parties in Norwegian countries, for instance, voluntarily adopted policies that require gender parity in selecting candidates. Argentina has had success with a national law that requires political parties to run women for at least 30 percent of their candidates. Before the law went into effect, about 5 percent of Argentinian lawmakers were women. After the law went into effect in 1993, women won 14 percent of the seats in the national chamber (Schwindt-Bayer 2009). Today, Argentina has a female president and women make up 37 percent of all legislators, putting this nation near the top of countries in the world in terms of gender equity in politics (QP 2013). Iceland, Norway, and Spain have recently taken this idea to a new level by requiring that women fill 40 percent of the seats on corporate boards of directors for major businesses based in their countries[3] (Teigen 2012). While all these policies seem far-fetched in America, their existence in other nations tells us that such achievements are possible.

But creating new policies that require gender parity in business or politics cannot be realized without a powerful feminist movement fighting for them. Nor will it be possible, more broadly, to achieve a society that respects and fulfills women's human rights. But challenging male-dominance is something that both women and men can take up wherever they are, in what whatever social organizations they are part of, such as the family, clubs, sports, churches, the workplace, the media, and politics. Since the resurrection of the women's movement in the 1960s, millions of Americans have been fighting for human rights as women's rights. It will take millions more in order to achieve their complete fulfillment and to create a truly equitable society.

DISCUSSION QUESTIONS

1. Going back to the Universal Declaration of Human Rights, identify which specific rights are at risk of being violated or left unfulfilled for many women in the United States. Be sure to explain your thinking.
2. We saw in the course of this chapter that sexual assaults are not committed in a bubble, but have much to do with social context. Please consider the social context of your campus or community. Are there certain factors you can identify that might elevate risks faced by women?
3. For the remainder of this day, try to pay attention to the objectification of bodies in the media you watch, for instance on your computer, TV, or in magazines. Are women's bodies objectified much more then men's bodies? Is the objectification of men's and women's bodies fundamentally the same, or is this objectification much different for men and women when it occurs in a sexist society like our own?
4. Throughout this book, we have seen that rights only become fulfilled when groups organize and develop the collective power necessary to challenge existing social relations. Based on what we've discussed in this chapter, how has the women's movement achieved important human rights victories in U.S. history? What kinds of victories do you think a future women's movement could win?

Notes

1 While men may be raped, the rate of victimization is much lower, about 1 in 71.
2 The United States by and large has a very poor track record on ratifying international human rights treaties. It has, however, ratified some important treaties like the International Covenant on Civil and Political Rights, the Convention Against All Forms of Racial Discrimination, and the International Convention Against Torture.
3 Today, women make up about 16 percent of corporate board members in the United States.

VI: U.S. Society, Global Inequalities, and Human Rights

～～✕～～

Please take out your cell phone. I'm not going to ask you to turn it off so it won't distract you from this text, although that's probably a good idea. What I would like you to do is to take a moment to consider how this slim little device links you to the rest of the world. And I'm not just talking about its capacity to cruise the internet or call and send messages to people across the globe, although that truly is remarkable. What I'm talking about is the very construction of your device, its physical components and the process by which it was put together. For example, all cell phones these days use a category of elements called rare earth minerals, which actually aren't all that rare at all, but they are hardly ever found in concentrated amounts that can be profitably mined. The United States once produced rare earth minerals at a mine in California, but it was closed down because it produced a large amount of radioactive waste that began leaking from storage facilities (Oskin 2013). Though this mine has recently been reopened, right now the vast majority of rare earth minerals in our cell phones and other computers come from China, where the government has used police power to crush citizen protests over levels of environmental contamination caused by rare earth mining that would not be tolerated in the United States (Downey, Bonds, and Clark 2010).

Our cell phones also use small amounts of the uncommon minerals palladium and platinum in their electrical circuitry, the mining of which is also extremely destructive and mostly done overseas. Our platinum, for instance, largely comes from South Africa, where miners work in harsh conditions to remove riches from underground, which are then shuttled off to global markets. The miners and their families often live in slum conditions that have improved little since the end of apartheid, with limited electricity and sanitation for their homes and few educational opportunities for their children (Essa 2013). And when these miners and other community groups protest, they are sometimes greeted with police violence reminiscent of the days of apartheid. In August of 2012, for instance, police opened fire at miners striking at a platinum mine in Marikana, killing 34 workers and wounding dozens more. What's more, the police then arrested 270 miners, accusing them of inciting violence that led to the death of their coworkers (Polgreen 2012). Conditions are of course different in Russia, which produces most of the palladium we use, largely from a single mining region and smelter at Norilsk, Siberia that was first built in the 1940s using communist-era forced labor. The pollution there is extensive, producing more toxic sulfur dioxide than the entire nation of France. While it's reported that conditions are too toxic for trees to grow for miles around the smelter, the actual extent of the pollution is impossible to know because the Russian government limits the reporting and scientific study that can be done there (Bonds and Downey 2012).

Finally, our cell phones all use an uncommon mineral named tantalum in their electrical circuitry. While much of this tantalum comes from either Australia or Brazil, some of it also comes from the eastern region of the Democratic Republic of the Congo (DRC). The decades-long conflict that has plagued this region, resulting in millions of deaths and the terrible mistreatment of civilians, is one of the great trage-dies of our time. The conditions that started this war and that sustain it are numerous and complex. Sadly, our global hunger for tantalum and other minerals in the Congo is one of these factors. Tantalum mines in the DRC can be dug by hand and provide an important source of income for armed groups to buy guns, munitions, and other tools used for making war (ICG 2012). Consequently, the government of the DRC and armed rebel groups fight with one another over the mines, and use them to sustain their fighting elsewhere in the region.

Taking all this together then, the physical components of our cell phones link us to human rights concerns around the world, and this says nothing about the labor condi-tions in factories where our cell phones are actually assembled. As you may be aware, there are human rights concerns here too. A Taiwanese company called Foxconn, which makes iPhones and iPads as well as other smart phones for Nokia and Motorola, has drawn the most public attention, not necessarily because its labor practices are worse compared to other electronics manufacturing companies, but due to its huge size. It employs 1.2 million workers in China alone (Duhigg and Barboza 2012). Prominent investigations of Foxconn in China have revealed that workers there are, not surprisingly, paid relatively low wages—just pennies on the dollar compared to the valuable products they work to produce. But perhaps more worrying, investigations have reported unsafe conditions—for instance the company requires some workers to stand for 10-hour days while others are exposed to toxic chemicals. The workweek at Foxconn is reported to be very long, stretching typically from 60 to 70 hours (Garside 2012). When the workday is over, Foxconn employees usually live at the factory, in dorm rooms that may hold has many as nine persons per room (Duhigg and Barboza 2012). The United States and other Western reporters first became aware of these labor conditions in 2010, after 14 Foxconn employees committed suicide at the facto-ries where they worked.

So looking again at your cell phone, think back and see if you can remember that almost magical moment when you opened it up its package and held it for the first time. Didn't it seem almost pristine? So shiny and polished smooth, somehow untouched by human hands. We know, of course, that this was an illusion. The phone that we use every day is material evidence of a very real relationship we have with people around the globe, even if these relationships typically remain unseen and unacknowledged. This poses a real challenge in regard to human rights. If you had personally traveled to the place where the tantalum or palladium in your phone came from to meet the miners, or if you visited the factory where your phone was assembled, you might be willing to pay a little extra to ensure that human rights are being respected along the production process, and you might even take political action to pressure companies to respect human rights and to encourage politicians to create new laws requiring this to happen. But our human relationships with people around the world don't appear to us as such, but, as Karl Marx wrote, these relationships appear to us as "things," even if they are highly advanced things that are themselves amazing technological feats. In this chapter we will explore our global interconnections and consider their human rights implications in the context of the contemporary world economy. We'll close by examining the strategies some groups have used in attempts to promote human wellbeing across nations.

Human Rights in the Global Economy

In his beautiful book *The Open Veins of Latin America*, Uruguayan historian and writer Eduardo Galeano (1973) gives us the image of Potosí, a city that was founded in the mid-16th century in Bolivia to mine the incredible riches from the nearby mountain, Cerro Rico. Despite being located at 13,000 feet above sea level, the city for a while became one of the largest in the Americas due to the vast richness of its silver mine. Over the centuries, literally thousands of tons of silver were removed from the mine. Little of this wealth, however, stayed. Most of the actual mining was conducted by forced Indian labor, and then by labor from African slaves brought to extract the silver ore. So to say the least, this labor process caused tremendous suffering and took a huge toll on local populations, rather than contributing to the economic development of the region. The actual silver was shipped off to Spain and what was formerly known as Great Britain (now the United Kingdom). What's left is a city with much poverty and a hollowed-out mountain, the surface of which has been mostly denuded of its native vegetation.

The image of Potosí is useful because it provides several reminders. First, while we hear a great deal about **globalization** in regard to recent developments in transnational economic production, thinking about Potosí helps us remember that since the very emergence of **colonialism** and the development of capitalism, economic production has spanned the Earth. After all, much of the raw materials that fueled and funded the Industrial Revolution in Western Europe, and then in the United States, came from the **Global South**, such as cotton, timber, rubber, gold, and silver from Africa and the Americas. So when scholars discuss "globalization" today, they are typically describing a new phase in the world economy, in which transnational production has become intensified and companies have become increasingly mobile. In a U.S. or European context, "globalization" is also often what we mean when we are thinking about **deindustrialization**, which is a process begun in the 1970s when transnational corporations began moving their factories from the Global North to take advantage of cheaper labor in the Global South.

Today, of course, the U.S. economy is completely dependent upon materials from overseas. One way to think about this is in terms of **critical minerals**, that are used to create the technologies and infrastructure of everyday life (see Table 6.1). There are no known replacements for these minerals, and while they are necessary for our American way of life, they overwhelmingly come from overseas (NRC 2008). As we've already discussed, rare earths are necessary for our electronics, but they come primarily from China. And we might not think much about the relatively recent aesthetic revolution in which all our television and computer screens became flat and our laptops became very thin, but this is due to the remarkable properties of a mineral called indium, which is not produced in the United States and primarily comes from Asia. So capitalism always has been and remains global. And we can see from the example of critical minerals that much of the technology and infrastructure of the contemporary economies in the Global North is built with materials from the Global South.

Additionally, the image of Potosí reminds us that global economic production has never been equitable and mutually beneficial to all the parties involved. Rather when global production networks draw resources and manufactured products from the regions in the Global South, it often involves a process of **underdevelopment**, in which great wealth is removed but little lasting value is added to local communities. Potosí was not "developed" through the establishment of the silver mine at Cerro

Table 6.1 Origins and Uses of Critical Minerals

Mineral	Uses	% of World Production
Platinum	Electronics and pollution control	South Africa (77%), Russia (13%), Canada (4%), Zimbabwe (2%), United States (2%)
Palladium	Electronics and pollution control	Russia (44%), South Africa (38%), United States (6%), Canada (6%), Zimbabwe (3%)
Rare earth elements	Computers and electronics	China (76%), France (9%), Japan (4%), Russia (3%), other (8%)
Manganese	Steel and cast iron	South Africa (19%), Australia (18%), China (13%), Brazil (12%), Gabon (11%)
Indium	Flat screens and computer display panels	China (60%), Japan (9%), South Korea (9%), Canada (9%), Belgium (5%)
Niobium	Building materials for aircraft and weapons	Brazil (90%), Canada (9%)
Vanadium	Building materials for aircraft and weapons	South Africa (39%), Canada (31%), Russia (27%)

Source: Downey, Bonds, and Clark (2010) "Natural Resource Extraction, Armed Violence, and Environmental Degradation."

Rico, so much as a whole region was underdeveloped as valuable minerals ultimately worth billions of dollars were pulled out and shipped far away, using the cheapest methods available, and leaving little in the way of investment for future economic production. This should not be a surprise, as this exploitative relationship was inherently part of the colonial experience.

However, relationships of underdevelopment did not end with the formal relationships of colonialism, but persist today. We might look, for instance, at Nigeria and its substantial oil production. The nation is the top oil exporter in Africa, producing almost 2.5 million barrels of oil a day, practically all of which is exported overseas. This oil, to say the least, is extremely valuable, grossing close to $90 billion a year (OPEC 2012). However, while this revenue has produced a few extremely wealthy Nigerians and helped enrich a broader national elite, most Nigerians have benefited very little from their nation's oil wealth. Poverty, in fact, has been growing. It's estimated that 61 percent of all Nigerians live in absolute poverty, sustaining themselves on incomes of less than a dollar a day (BBC 2012). Global networks of production have, in other words, underdeveloped Nigeria, removing much of its oil wealth that might have been used to fund education, healthcare, or that simply might have been used as a source of domestic fuel to drive other kinds of economic production in the future. What many Nigerians have gotten instead is a conflict-ridden society, as groups fight over the uneven distribution of the money it generates, along with a tremendous amount of environmental degradation.

The extent to which manufacturing and apparel production can contribute to the fulfillment of human rights in the Global South, or whether it will constitute another form of underdevelopment, is a complicated question. On the one hand, many nations hope that by attracting multinational corporations to their shores to invest in factories to make clothes, shoes, and electronics for global consumption, they will get much in return, including much needed jobs and an opportunity to spur economic growth. Often, however, countries may compete with one another to offer transnational companies the lowest rates of taxation, the lowest wages, and the fewest environmental and worker protections. This **global race to the bottom** means that multinational corporations can pick and choose between countries in order to find the cheapest rates of production. And after selecting a location, if the costs of production begin increasing, they can always choose to move again. Such a global context has proved to be a recipe for underdevelopment in many nations rather than a means to increase wellbeing for their citizens as a whole.

Historically, these processes of underdevelopment were achieved through the military power of colonizing nations. Today, terms of **unequal exchange** are typically achieved through other means. To begin with, the history of colonialism is not that old. It wasn't until the 1950s, 1960s, and 1970s that many previously colonized areas in Africa, Asia, and the Caribbean achieved independence. When these nations became independent, their economies and political systems had been malformed by centuries of imperial governance (Wallerstein 2004). Their economies were geared toward the exploitation of raw materials and cheap labor for external markets, and they had very little infrastructure in place that could be used for the betterment of their societies.

The international financial organizations that were created at the end of World War II didn't help much, either. The **World Bank**, for instance, is an institution that was created to fund economic development projects in the Global South in order to reduce poverty. In practice, the World Bank has historically funded megaprojects like big dams and big mines that are very profitable to multinational companies, but often-times end up hurting local people as much as helping them (Goldman 2006). World Bank-funded gold mines in Ghana, for instance, have displaced thousands of people from their homes and cropland, while piling up massive amounts of toxic waste and contaminating drinking water. Moreover, few members in the communities adjacent to mines have gotten jobs due to the high degree of mechanization in modern mineral extraction (McCarthy 2011).

Along with the World Bank, the **International Monetary Fund** (or IMF) was created to promote global economic security by providing short-lived loans to nations experiencing financial difficulties, in hopes that those difficulties would not ripple throughout world markets. In practice, the IMF has indeed provided loans to nations in the Global South, but they have often been given with conditions that require recipient nations to undertake reforms that are at odds with human rights, for instance by reducing public expenditures on education or healthcare (Blau and Moncado 2009). According to many critics of the contemporary global economy, these financial institutions, along with the dynamics of the "global race to the bottom," have worked to maintain unequal terms of trade between nations even after the end of formal colonial rule. While these relationships have been around for a long time, they are not, of course, necessarily permanent. Things can change, and many people throughout the world are pushing to change them sooner rather than later in ways that advance global human rights.

Efforts to Promote Global Human Rights

It's clear that we live in a very interconnected world, and that we cannot easily separate ourselves from human rights violations in other countries, especially when they provide some of the food, minerals, and labor that make our daily lives possible. But what people in the Global North can do to promote wellbeing rights in other nations is not an easy question to answer. Some human rights innovators have sought to use the relative privilege and the purchasing power of U.S. consumers as a force for good by creating **Fair Trade** certification. The goal is to create market incentives in order to encourage producers of goods destined for U.S. or European markets to respect labor rights, to pay a living wage, and to contribute to community development. When producers adhere to these standards, a third-party organization like Fair Trade USA certifies them and gives them a fair trade label to use on their products. With the proper education, the hope goes, U.S. and European consumers will be willing to pay a little extra to buy fair trade-labeled products knowing that their coffee, bananas, chocolate, or whatever else were not produced under abusive conditions, but instead under conditions that respected and improved people's wellbeing.

Over the past 15 years, fair trade certified production has shown surprising growth, even in the midst of the global economic slowdown that began in late 2007. Today, Fair Trade products account for $700 million in global trade (Elliot 2012). Fair Trade USA (2013: 5) reports that there is "continued growth in consumer demand for almost 12,000 Fair Trade Certified products now available in virtually every major supermarket in America as well as thousands of restaurants, cafeterias and cafés." It is clear that Fair Trade production has helped improve the lives of thousands, if not hundreds of thousands of persons around the world in sometimes quite profound ways (Fair Trade USA 2013). For those consumers who are able to afford it and are willing to pay a little extra, buying fair trade certified products is an important way to help promote human rights throughout the world.

But that, of course, is the major hitch. As we've discussed in previous chapters, a large number of Americans are struggling just to get by. And even for those technically able to afford it, many Americans may not feel like they can pay extra, given that their incomes, on average, have been stagnating or declining for several decades now. Consequently, fair trade products remain a niche market, accounting for just a drop in the bucket of global commerce between the Global South and the Global North. For instance, while coffee is the most successful fair trade certified product, in terms of the total revenue it produces, it only accounts for 2 percent of the U.S. market (Elliot 2012).

Some activists have recognized the limitations of relying on individual consumers in order to promote fair trade, and have since sought to create policy changes in order to achieve more just global trade relationships. In the mid-1990s, for instance, many university students became very concerned that their high-priced clothing was being produced in overseas sweatshops where employees worked long hours in poor and unsafe conditions for little money. Rather than trying to change these conditions through their individual purchasing power, students mounted campaigns to pressure their universities to ensure that clothing that carried a university logo was certified as being produced under conditions that protected workers' rights. Students across the country at all kinds of universities and colleges convinced their schools to comply, sometimes even resorting to sit-ins at administrators' offices and going on hunger strikes (Featherstone 2002). Ultimately, the impact was mixed. While the certification scheme did help some workers, any improvements were dwarfed by the vast scale of the global assembly line, which has remained unchanged (Seidman 2009). But certainly, these students' collective action made more impact than what would have been possible through their individual purchasing decisions alone.

More recently, activists successfully pushed the U.S. Congress to require electronics manufacturers to publicly disclose if any of the minerals used to produce their computers originally came from the Democratic Republic of the Congo. As a result, rather than being accused of using "blood minerals," companies are working to find alternative sources (Wilkie 2013). It remains to be seen, however, if this law can help stem the terrible violence in the DRC, or the trade in valuable minerals that has helped fuel it.

Many activists concerned about global justice are, however, very skeptical of efforts to advance rights through consumerism or policy changes within wealthier nations like the United States. These activists instead place much more emphasis on the potential for **social movements** rooted in the Global South to transform both local and international politics to create a more equitable world order. Consequently, they try to find ways to support and partner with Global South movements, for instance by attending and participating in the World Social Forum, which is an annual event held since 2001 that attracts tens of thousands of global justice activists from around the world to debate strategy and inspire change (Smith and Wiest 2012). The goal of the World Social Forum is to create a broad coalition comprised of thousands of grassroots organizations—a "movement of movements"—to challenge the inequitable structure of the world economy. To what extent it can have any transformative impact is, of course, yet to be seen. But some social scientists and human rights activists take hope in the fact that social movements have never been so interconnected as they are today, along with the fact that our particular historical moment seems to be one of significant social change, as we will discuss in the next chapter (Wallerstein 2004). The direction of this change is not yet determined, but global justice activists hope to push it towards the greater fulfillment of human rights.

DISCUSSION QUESTIONS

1. In this chapter you were asked to consider the global human rights implications of the production of your cell phone. But this was only one example used to illustrate global inequalities and the ways that our contemporary economic system is tilted in favor of nations in the Global North. See if you can replicate this example, by for instance doing some internet research to learn about the production of the blue jeans you are wearing, or about the production of the ingredients for the chocolate bar or fruit smoothie you might buy for yourself today as a reward for reading this chapter.

2. Global inequalities were once maintained primarily through the violence of colonial relationships. How, according to this chapter, have these inequalities been built into the contemporary world order, and how are they maintained today?

3. In this chapter, we considered three main ways global justice activists in wealthier nations like the United States have sought to promote human rights in the Global South. Which of these do you think might be the most effective? Are there any that seem destined to fail? Is it possible that all three strategies could be used simultaneously, or are they mutually exclusive? Please explain your answer.

VII: Conclusion: Volunteerism, Activism, and the Pursuit of Human Rights

Sometimes we in the United States like to tell ourselves comfortable myths about the origins of progressive social change. In one story, for instance, we like to think that politicians ultimately decided to abolish Jim Crow segregation because they were swept up in a broader cultural transformation happening across our country, being spurred on by the eloquence and wisdom of civil rights leaders like Dr. Martin Luther King Jr. While there certainly is truth in the idea that changes in people's thinking and attitudes can instigate broader changes in the priorities of governments, sociologists who have studied the Civil Rights Movement argue that the story is much more complicated. For example, conventional narratives of the Civil Rights Movement overlook the real person of Dr. King by glossing over the fact that he wasn't simply on a mission to promote "diversity" in American institutions and did not only challenge legally codified racism, but also sought to challenge the ways that racism was embedded in the U.S. economy (Dyson 2001). Dr. King was also a strong critic of the Vietnam War and expressed a vision for the fundamental transformation of the United States in order to achieve justice, peace, and equality both at home and around the world (King 1967).

The typical stories we tell ourselves about social change also mislead us into thinking that the Civil Rights victories came from the top down, rather than the bottom up. But sociologists who have studied the Civil Rights movement stress that politicians did not end segregation because it was the right thing to do, but because thousands of people at the grassroots level were working in different ways—pushing, pressing, and putting their bodies on the line—to force otherwise reluctant politicians to act (McAdam 1983). The main lesson here is that in very few instances in U.S. society do elected politicians work—as leaders, and on their own accord—to further human rights. But with this said, grassroots movements can sometimes compel them to do so, and when this happens governments can enact laws and create institutions that enhance human wellbeing. In this chapter we will consider how grassroots movements can work to propel advances in human rights, and we will situate such work within our particular historical moment, which is one that is tumultuous and seems as if it could move toward either a hopeful or more menacing future in regard to the human condition. First, however, we will discuss the importance and limitations of volunteerism as a kind of human rights work.

Volunteering to Fulfill Human Rights

When learning about a social problem, many people—for obvious reasons—feel the need to do something about it. For many, volunteering in one's community is the best place to start. Indeed, volunteer-based **nonprofit organizations** do absolutely crucial human rights work in every city, town, and rural outpost throughout the United States. In my own town, for instance, a coalition of church groups works to run the only homeless shelter. The coalition also provides an open kitchen that hands out free breakfasts and lunches, and also creates opportunities for free health screenings. Volunteers, moreover, help run the local food bank, which provides donated food to low-income and jobless community members that might otherwise go without. And it's a nonprofit organization that, again running largely on volunteer power, works to provide support to victims of rape and sexual assault. And through the work of volunteers—many of them college students—community organizations help tutor students from low-income households. All of this work is clearly being done in order to help fulfill basic human rights in my community. Undoubtedly, my town, and the United States as a whole, would be a much colder, much more cruel place without people's voluntary efforts to promote and fulfill the human rights of others.

Volunteerism is a celebrated aspect of U.S. culture. Even conservative activists and politicians who are working to end or scale back government programs that feed, house, and educate the poor don't really want to see these fundamental human rights go unfilled. They just believe that this shouldn't be the work of the government and that it shouldn't consume tax dollars. Instead, they argue, this work should be the province of churches and other community groups. The question, of course, is whether or not volunteerism is sufficient. The Declaration of Human Rights was written, of course, from the perspective that it clearly is not. The scale of need in terms of housing, education, and medicine is so vast that governments are the only social institutions that have the capacity to deliver to those in need. Moreover, as we've seen, achieving human rights often means challenging vested interests that privilege some while disadvantaging others. In democratic societies, governments can play a necessary role as arbiter between conflicting interests and as an enforcer of new laws that dismantle old oppressions and promote wellbeing.

To talk about the essential role of governments in promoting human rights is not to belittle or dismiss volunteerism in any way. In the contemporary United States, volunteerism is critically important for those in need. Moreover, it provides a way through which volunteers can work to improve the lives of real individuals while contributing more broadly to their communities as a whole. And it gives volunteers a chance to make new connections and bridge divides across race and class while gaining greater insight about the city or town where they live. Additionally, it provides a way that we can live up to our personal or religious beliefs about what it means to be a good person, allowing us to earn both self-respect and the respect of others.

Nonetheless, volunteerism ultimately is not enough. Those that work directly with the poor through religious or community groups will often tell you as much themselves. Achieving the full range of human rights in U.S. society requires a change in what governments do. State and federal governments in the United States, however, have typically been reluctant to make changes in laws and policies to fulfill human rights, unless, that is, they are faced with extraordinary pressure from below. For this reason, work to build grassroots pressure to change government policy is also an important form of human rights work in the United States.

Taking Political Action to Promote Human Rights

The ability to cast a vote in elections and the ability to freely express one's political views are fundamental human rights. However, as we've seen in Chapter III, given the huge amounts of money that are necessary to influence politics in the United States, the actual impact of these rights is often quite limited in terms of shaping what our government does and does not do. For this reason, many human rights proponents—whether they call themselves this or not—take up **activism** by working to influence politics outside the traditional arenas of voting and campaign finance. The major ways activists work to create change is through legal strategies, cultural strategies, and nonviolent protest. While social movement campaigns typically employ all three strategies simultaneously, they often come to rely on one method more than others, depending upon the resources they have available and the political environment they are operating in.

The contemporary Gay and Lesbian Movement, for instance, has made use of all three strategies. Initially in many American cities, for instance, the movement often engaged in high profile and disruptive tactics in an attempt to challenge heterosexist policies that targeted or excluded people who do not abide by conventional gender norms (Bernstein 1997). More recently, the movement has had tremendous success utilizing a **legal strategy of social change** to challenge laws banning same sex marriages as unconstitutional. While gay and lesbian activists began filing lawsuits in the 1970s to gain the right to marry, the approach did not begin to make waves until the 1990s when the Hawaiian State Supreme Court ruled that a ban on same sex unions was unconstitutional (Stolberg 2013). And while citizens in Hawaii amended their constitution through a referendum to outlaw same sex marriage, a tactic that would be used by foes of same sex marriage in other states, ultimately the legal strategies used by the Gay and Lesbian Movement have been very successful.

In 2003 the movement won a watershed legal victory when the Massachusetts State Supreme Court ruled in favor of gay and lesbian advocates, declaring that laws barring same sex marriage created second-class citizens, something forbidden by the state constitution (Stolberg 2013). Other legal challenges were filed against a California constitutional amendment barring same sex marriage and against a federal law—the

1993 Defense of Marriage Act—that does the same. Both challenges were ultimately victorious and, establishing a powerful legal precedent for gay and lesbian rights, were eventually upheld by the U.S. Supreme Court in 2013.

It's of course an oversimplification to credit the Gay and Lesbian Movement's legal advocacy for its recent success because social movements are diverse and are made up of many organizations that stress different kinds of tactics. And there certainly are organizations across the nation working to change public opinion about same sex marriage and gay and lesbian rights more generally, but the Gay and Lesbian Movement has placed a major emphasis in achieving human rights by challenging unjust laws. As their legal victories mounted, other efforts to change American's attitudes about gay marriage gained more traction and more and more people began to agree. Consequently, some states have begun to legalize same sex marriage through legislation and public referendums, beginning first with Maine, Maryland, and Washington in 2012. These victories are some of the most salient advancements in human rights in the United States in recent years.

Since the 1960s, and the beginnings of what is referred to as the **Second Wave** of the U.S. Women's Movement, feminist activists have also utilized a range of tactics, including the use of lawsuits challenging discriminatory laws and efforts to mount disruptive protests. But the Women's Movement has possibly been most successful through a **cultural strategy of social change** by transforming women's understandings about themselves and their world. In the 1960s and 1970s women across America formed **consciousness-raising groups**, local women's support networks, and feminist bookstores (Burns 1990). This was an effort for women to begin talking with one another to understand the commonality of their experiences, that for instance being subjected to sexual assault, sexual harassment, and job discrimination were not the result of individual decisions, just as it wasn't the result of their individual decisions that they lost personal autonomy or were unfairly burdened by work at home. Rather, these were shared experiences common to countless numbers of women and were ultimately the consequence of living in a sexist society. Consciousness-raising groups and grassroots women's organizations aimed to make the personal political by proposing that a different kind of society and a different kind of life was possible. By so doing, the Women's Movement empowered women to stand up against sexism in their personal spheres, whether it was in the family or the workplace, and to raise children with different kinds of expectations and with much broader horizons about what women can achieve.

Like the Women's and the Gay and Lesbian Movements, US Blacks have long utilized both legal and cultural strategies to promote rights, pioneered by the **NAACP**. This civil rights organization was founded in 1909 in order to end segregation and the common practice of lynching and other forms of white mob violence directed against black communities. The legal strategies of the NAACP were pivotal in the early years of the Civil Rights Movement, especially in the landmark 1954 victory of

Brown vs. Board of Education, in which the U.S. Supreme Court ruled in favor of the Black litigants challenging school segregation. It was, however, the use of disruptive **nonviolence** where Civil Rights Movement organizations made previous legal and political victories real in the lives of Blacks. Building from the successful use of non-violence in South Africa and India, the goal of this strategy was to provoke a crisis in U.S. society that would compel reluctant white federal lawmakers in Washington D.C. to intervene in the politics of Southern states in order to force them to recognize the basic civil and political rights of African Americans (McAdam 1983).

Black Civil Rights leaders strategically chose to mount community-wide protests in Birmingham, Alabama, for instance, knowing that the Chief of Police Bull Connor would react brutally to peaceful protesters (Burns 1990). The resulting protests and the violence committed by authorities paralyzed the city of Birmingham and forced local business owners and politicians to cede to some of the movement's demands. More significantly, the images of fire houses and police dogs being used against peaceful protesters, including children, were spread across the world and compelled the otherwise recalcitrant Kennedy and Johnson presidential administrations to press for and ultimately sign into law the Civil Rights Act, which outlaws racial discrimination.

Taking these three examples together, it's clear that legal, cultural, and nonviolence strategies are all used by social movement organizations working to advance human rights in the United States, and that individual movements will come to stress one of these strategies over others as they assess what resources they have available (like money, access to lawyers, people willing to protest and go to jail, etc.) and what the political environment looks like in their particular situation (such as the presence of sympathetic judges, vulnerable politicians and other elites, or the extent of police repression). Regardless of the particular strategies in question, however, the larger point is that social movement activism was necessary to win fundamental human rights for gays and lesbians, women, and Blacks in U.S. society. Historically, gains in human rights have not simply come about because granting them seemed like a good thing to do. Gains were made because people fought for them, often times at great personal sacrifice.

This is an important lesson to remember as we evaluate U.S. society from a human rights perspective today. In the course of this book we have measured our nation in terms of the goals and ideals set forth in the Universal Declaration of Human Rights, and we have found that in many important ways it comes up short. We, as a nation, can do better in terms of human rights. But doing better won't be easy. Even if we all ultimately suffer in the long term when human rights are violated or are otherwise left unfilled, at least in the short term some individuals do benefit. White people benefit from historic and contemporary racism. Men benefit from sexism. The very wealthy benefit, at least initially, when their riches are not taxed at high enough rates to fund governmental programs to provide wellbeing rights to the poor, and when large businesses are not compelled to pay workers wages that would allow them to purchase things like adequate nutrition and healthcare for their families.

Working to promote human rights now and in the future will mean challenging this system of privileges and benefits that has been entrenched within our social structure. For those who take up this work, it will mean filing lawsuits, engaging in arguments and working to change people's attitudes, and even protesting and—for some—risking arrest or suffering other costs. It will mean forging ahead even when people say, "I agree with you, but now's not the time." It will mean making waves and being noisy even when some advise, "I agree with you, but please calm down." This is what King's (1963) famous "Letter from a Birmingham Jail" is all about, when sympathetic white religious leaders publically encouraged him to be patient and forgo disruptive tactics. King, of course, famously answered back that, "history is the long and tragic story of the fact that privileged groups seldom give up their privileges voluntarily." Waiting for privileged groups to negotiate about their unearned rewards effectively means waiting forever, that is until activists are able and willing, according to King, "to create a situation so crisis-packed that it will inevitably open the door to negotiation." Kings words echo those of another human rights hero from America's past, the former slave and abolitionist leader Frederick Douglas (1857), who said that "if there is no struggle there is no progress. Those who profess to favor freedom and yet depreciate agitation, are men who want crops without plowing up the ground, they want rain without thunder and lightening. They want the ocean without the awful roar of its many waters."

Human Rights, Turbulent Times, and our Uncertain Future

Steven Pinker (2012), an evolutionary psychologist by training, likes to think about the big picture in terms of human history. And in that big picture, he writes, people have been treating each other much, much better, thanks in part to broad cultural changes he calls the "rights revolution." It is instructive to remember, according to Pinker, that before the turn of the last century, lynchings and white mob violence against African Americans was far from infrequent. Additionally, women and children enjoyed few legal rights and could be abused by husbands and fathers with impunity. Finally, it's worth remembering that not so long ago gay and lesbian Americans could be victimized by groups of thugs or harassed and thrown into prisons or psychiatric wards by police. Thanks to the Civil Rights, the Women's, and the Gay and Lesbian Movements—all bound up in a larger rights revolution—the United States has come a long way. This, perhaps, is what Martin Luther King Jr. meant when he famously said in 1965 that "the arc of the moral universe is long, but it bends toward justice."

This is a compelling image, and one that is rooted in Dr. King's spiritual worldview. But as sociologists we must recognize that there is nothing inevitable about social progress toward the increasing fulfillment of human rights. Unfortunately, reversals on the road to human rights are equally possible. Indeed, the contemporary global economy has been beset by a number of challenges since the collapse of the U.S. housing market in 2007. For several decades, beginning in the late 1940s, the United States had the predominant economy in the world, able to produce better products, more products, and less expensive products than businesses in other nations. Since the late 1970s, however, American manufacturers increasingly left the United States, seeking out cheaper labor. On top of this, the increasing **automation of work** has meant that the same levels of production now require fewer workers. Despite the loss of manufacturing jobs, people in the United States continued to be the consumers of the world well into the 1990s and 2000s, buying products and fueling the demand for more manufacturing from companies operating across the globe. The collapse of the American housing market showed, however, that U.S. consumers had recently been spending money they didn't really have. This realization rippled across the world economy, triggering banking collapses and shuttering businesses in its wake.

Today, the global economy has yet to fully recover. While the U.S. economy is now slowly growing, economic inequality is also increasing and the median income for U.S. workers in 2013 remains six percent less than its 2007 level (Pear 2013). Europe's economy, meanwhile, has stagnated and economic growth in the Global South has remained subdued compared to levels before the recession. The fundamental problem facing the nations of the world is that the global economy can produce far more goods and services than people can afford, either because they are jobless or because they are being paid too little. But without increasing rates of consumption, there is little incentive for companies to make investments that would create jobs and increase rates of economic growth. The result is a long-term economic stupor that has put wellbeing rights at risk in many nations around the world, and in some cases it has even resulted in some significant declines.

Soon after the global economy entered into recession, a wave of large protest movements erupted that sent political shockwaves around the world. First there were massive protests in late 2010 in Greece and Tunisia (sparking what has come to be known as the Arab Spring), followed up by protests in Egypt, Libya, and Syria that ultimately transformed those nations. Riots, non-violent occupations, and mass protest marches then broke out in Spain, the United Kingdom, Russia, and—through the Occupy Movement—in the United States. Continuing further, grassroots uprisings upended politics in both Turkey and Brazil as late as 2013.

The causes of these protests are diverse and dependent upon local circumstances, according to journalist Paul Mason (2013) who has traveled around the world documenting these events, but they also share some common features. First, all these protest movements have been made up of three primary groups: by college students and young professionals—who have mostly led the charge—that are facing a future with lower pay and higher rates of joblessness compared to previous generations; by members of the more traditional labor movement; and by the ranks of the unemployed or the otherwise very poor. Second, according to Mason, these movements have all shared a somewhat spontaneous origin, made possible because people have become more and more interconnected through cell phones and social networking sites like Facebook and Twitter.

Ultimately, the consequences of this global revolt have been mixed and it is too soon to know exactly how much change they created. In Egypt, the uprising brought down one authoritarian government but soon replaced it with another. In Syria, a pro-democracy uprising opened up tremendous social cleavages that tragically brought about a horrific civil war. While in Tunisia, the rebellion resulted in the establishment of a fragile—and far from perfect—democracy.

The impacts of this world revolt were felt outside the Middle East as well. One positive outcome in the United States is that it created an opportunity where we could, at least for a time, have more public conversations about the high rates of income and wealth inequality in our society, along with opening up more conversations about the declining prospects of our young people. In Brazil, the uprising pressured the government to propose reforms to limit corruption and to refocus government spending away from building huge soccer stadiums and other megaprojects, but to instead use government money to address real human needs (Dalbert 2013). In other nations, such as Greece and Russia, governments have responded to protests with harsh repression while simultaneously tolerating the rise of far-right movements that blame immigrants, people of color, and gays and lesbians for economic problems and "social decline" (Mason 2013).

This is the major risk ahead of us, that governments may prove unwilling or unable to address the causes of the ongoing global economic malaise while simultaneously continuing a global program of austerity by cutting public services. In response to the upwelling of popular protests, governments may restrict civil liberties—like the right to free assembly and the right to free speech—while partnering with political organizations that hope to return their societies to periods when male privilege and, depending upon the society we are discussing, white privilege was taken-for-granted and defended by the state (Robinson and Barrera 2012). In this way, contemporary declines in wellbeing rights may well be linked to future declines in civil and political rights in many nations throughout the world, including the United States.

But of course this particular future remains unwritten. And we all, as social actors ourselves, may like to have a say in it and work to influence its outcome. In the beginning of this text, we introduced the idea of human rights as both a morally grounded means of assessing wellbeing in societies while also being a political project, in the sense that human rights are a widely-shared set of aspirations toward which we might collectively strive in order to improve the human condition. This book has argued that the United States, when measured against human rights standards, fails to live up to our shared ideals about what people deserve in life. This book has also offered a number of different policy alternatives through which rights could be increasingly fulfilled. But the book has stressed that these policies won't enact themselves. Our contemporary historical moment offers both peril and potential in terms of human wellbeing. The choices we make today and the ways that we choose to incorporate or not incorporate human rights politics into our own lives will influence exactly what kind of future it is that we will share tomorrow.

DISCUSSION QUESTIONS

1.   According to this chapter, what is the importance of volunteerism in terms of the fulfillment of human rights in the United States? What are the limitations of volunteerism as a means of satisfying rights?
2.   Thinking back to a policy recommendation discussed in a previous chapter that might advance human rights in the United States, what social movement strategy discussed in this chapter—stressing either legal campaigns, efforts to change attitudes and values, or nonviolence—do you think would be the most effective way to advance it?
3.   Where do you see the greatest opportunities for the future advancement of human rights in the United States? Where do you see the biggest risks in terms of human rights reversals? Please explain your answer.
4.   This book closed by stating that human rights are necessarily political. What do you think this means? Does thinking about human rights work as a kind of politics change how you think about them? Why or why not?

Appendix: The Universal Declaration of Human Rights

～～✕～～

Whereas recognition of the inherent dignity and of the equal and inalienable rights of all members of the human family is the foundation of freedom, justice and peace in the world.

Whereas disregard and contempt for human rights have resulted in barbarous acts which have outraged the conscience of mankind, and the advent of a world in which human beings shall enjoy freedom of speech and belief and freedom from fear and want has been proclaimed as the highest aspiration of the common people.

Whereas it is essential, if man is not to be compelled to have recourse, as a last resort, to rebellion against tyranny and oppression, that human rights should be protected by the rule of law.

Whereas it is essential to promote the development of friendly relations between nations.

Whereas the peoples of the United Nations have in the Charter reaffirmed their faith in fundamental human rights, in the dignity and worth of the human person and in the equal rights of men and women and have determined to promote social progress and better standards of life in larger freedom.

Whereas Member States have pledged themselves to achieve, in co-operation with the United Nations, the promotion of universal respect for and observance of human rights and fundamental freedoms.

Whereas a common understanding of these rights and freedoms is of the greatest importance for the full realization of this pledge.

Now, Therefore THE GENERAL ASSEMBLY proclaims THIS UNIVERSAL DECLARATION OF HUMAN RIGHTS as a common standard of achievement for all peoples and all nations, to the end that every individual and every organ of society, keeping this Declaration constantly in mind, shall strive by teaching and education to promote respect for these rights and freedoms and by progressive measures, national and international, to secure their universal and effective recognition and observance, both among the peoples of Member States themselves and among the peoples of territories under their jurisdiction.

Article 1

All human beings are born free and equal in dignity and rights. They are endowed with reason and conscience and should act towards one another in a spirit of brotherhood.

Article 2

Everyone is entitled to all the rights and freedoms set forth in this Declaration, without distinction of any kind, such as race, colour, sex, language, religion, political or other opinion, national or social origin, property, birth or other status. Furthermore, no distinction shall be made on the basis of the political, jurisdictional or international status of the country or territory to which a person belongs, whether it be independent, trust, non-self-governing or under any other limitation of sovereignty.

Article 3

Everyone has the right to life, liberty and security of person.

Article 4

No one shall be held in slavery or servitude; slavery and the slave trade shall be prohibited in all their forms.

Article 5

No one shall be subjected to torture or to cruel, inhuman or degrading treatment or punishment.

Article 6

Everyone has the right to recognition everywhere as a person before the law.

Article 7

All are equal before the law and are entitled without any discrimination to equal protection of the law. All are entitled to equal protection against any discrimination in violation of this Declaration and against any incitement to such discrimination.

Article 8

Everyone has the right to an effective remedy by the competent national tribunals for acts violating the fundamental rights granted him by the constitution or by law.

Article 9

No one shall be subjected to arbitrary arrest, detention or exile.

Article 10

Everyone is entitled in full equality to a fair and public hearing by an independent and impartial tribunal, in the determination of his rights and obligations and of any criminal charge against him.

Article 11

1. Everyone charged with a penal offence has the right to be presumed innocent until proved guilty according to law in a public trial at which he has had all the guarantees necessary for his defence.
2. No one shall be held guilty of any penal offence on account of any act or omission which did not constitute a penal offence, under national or international law, at the time when it was committed. Nor shall a heavier penalty be imposed than the one that was applicable at the time the penal offence was committed.

Article 12

No one shall be subjected to arbitrary interference with his privacy, family, home or correspondence, nor to attacks upon his honour and reputation. Everyone has the right to the protection of the law against such interference or attacks.

Article 13

1. Everyone has the right to freedom of movement and residence within the borders of each state.
2. Everyone has the right to leave any country, including his own, and to return to his country.

Article 14

1. Everyone has the right to seek and to enjoy in other countries asylum from persecution.

2. This right may not be invoked in the case of prosecutions genuinely arising from non-political crimes or from acts contrary to the purposes and principles of the United Nations.

Article 15

1. Everyone has the right to a nationality.
2. No one shall be arbitrarily deprived of his nationality nor denied the right to change his nationality.

Article 16

1. Men and women of full age, without any limitation due to race, nationality or religion, have the right to marry and to found a family. They are entitled to equal rights as to marriage, during marriage and at its dissolution.
2. Marriage shall be entered into only with the free and full consent of the intending spouses.
3. The family is the natural and fundamental group unit of society and is entitled to protection by society and the State.

Article 17

1. Everyone has the right to own property alone as well as in association with others.
2. No one shall be arbitrarily deprived of his property.

Article 18

Everyone has the right to freedom of thought, conscience and religion; this right includes freedom to change his religion or belief, and freedom, either alone or in community with others and in public or private, to manifest his religion or belief in teaching, practice, worship and observance.

Article 19

Everyone has the right to freedom of opinion and expression; this right includes freedom to hold opinions without interference and to seek, receive and impart information and ideas through any media and regardless of frontiers.

Article 20

1. Everyone has the right to freedom of peaceful assembly and association.
2. No one may be compelled to belong to an association.

Article 21

1. Everyone has the right to take part in the government of his country, directly or through freely chosen representatives.
2. Everyone has the right of equal access to public service in his country.
3. The will of the people shall be the basis of the authority of government; this will shall be expressed in periodic and genuine elections which shall be by universal and equal suffrage and shall be held by secret vote or by equivalent free voting procedures.

Article 22

Everyone, as a member of society, has the right to social security and is entitled to realization, through national effort and international co-operation and in accordance with the organization and resources of each State, of the economic, social and cultural rights indispensable for his dignity and the free development of his personality.

Article 23

1. Everyone has the right to work, to free choice of employment, to just and favourable conditions of work and to protection against unemployment.
2. Everyone, without any discrimination, has the right to equal pay for equal work.
3. Everyone who works has the right to just and favourable remuneration ensuring for himself and his family an existence worthy of human dignity, and supplemented, if necessary, by other means of social protection.
4. Everyone has the right to form and to join trade unions for the protection of his interests.

Article 24

Everyone has the right to rest and leisure, including reasonable limitation of working hours and periodic holidays with pay.

Article 25

1. Everyone has the right to a standard of living adequate for the health and well-being of himself and of his family, including food, clothing, housing and medical

care and necessary social services, and the right to security in the event of unemployment, sickness, disability, widowhood, old age or other lack of livelihood in circumstances beyond his control.

2. Motherhood and childhood are entitled to special care and assistance. All children, whether born in or out of wedlock, shall enjoy the same social protection.

Article 26

1. Everyone has the right to education. Education shall be free, at least in the elementary and fundamental stages. Elementary education shall be compulsory. Technical and professional education shall be made generally available and higher education shall be equally accessible to all on the basis of merit.
2. Education shall be directed to the full development of the human personality and to the strengthening of respect for human rights and fundamental freedoms. It shall promote understanding, tolerance and friendship among all nations, racial or religious groups, and shall further the activities of the United Nations for the maintenance of peace.
3. Parents have a prior right to choose the kind of education that shall be given to their children.

Article 27

1. Everyone has the right freely to participate in the cultural life of the community, to enjoy the arts and to share in scientific advancement and its benefits.
2. Everyone has the right to the protection of the moral and material interests resulting from any scientific, literary or artistic production of which he is the author.

Article 28

Everyone is entitled to a social and international order in which the rights and freedoms set forth in this Declaration can be fully realized.

Article 29

1. Everyone has duties to the community in which alone the free and full development of his personality is possible.
2. In the exercise of his rights and freedoms, everyone shall be subject only to such limitations as are determined by law solely for the purpose of securing due

recognition and respect for the rights and freedoms of others and of meeting the just requirements of morality, public order and the general welfare in a democratic society.

3.   These rights and freedoms may in no case be exercised contrary to the purposes and principles of the United Nations.

Article 30

Nothing in this Declaration may be interpreted as implying for any State, group or person any right to engage in any activity or to perform any act aimed at the destruction of any of the rights and freedoms set forth herein.

References

99 Percent. 2011a. "We Are the 99 Percent" blog. Retrieved July 19, 2013 (http://wearethe99percent. tumblr.com/post/12924316464).

———— 2011b. "We Are the 99 Percent" blog. Retrieved July 19, 2013 (http://wearethe99percent. tumblr.com/post/14025801150/my-job-that-only-pays-me-30-000-year-requires-a).

———— 2011c. "We Are the 99 Percent" blog. Retrieved July 19, 2013 (http://wearethe99percent. tumblr.com/post/13204638078).

Abrams, Jim. 2010. "Congress Passes Bill to Reduce Disparity in Crack, Powder Cocaine Sentencing." *Washington Post*, July 29. Retrieved July 22, 2013 (http://www.washingtonpost.com/wp-dyn/ content/article/2010/07/28/AR2010072802969.html).

Agyeman, Julian. 2013. *Introducing Just Sustainabilities: Policy, Planning, and Practice*. London: Zed Books.

Alexander, Michele. 2012. *The New Jim Crow: Mass Incarceration in the Age of Colorblindness*. New York: The New Press.

Armaline, William T., Davita Silfen Glasberg, and Bandana Purkayastha (eds.) 2011. *Human Rights in our own Backyard: Injustice and Resistance in the United States*. Philadelphia: University of Pennsylvania Press.

Armstrong, Elizabeth A., Laura Hamilton, and Brian Sweeney. 2006. "Sexual Assault on Campus: A Multilevel, Integrative Approach to Party Rape." *Social Problems* 53: 483–99.

BBC. 2012. "Nigerians Living in Poverty Rise to Nearly 61%." *BBC News*, February 13. Retrieved August 26, 2013 (http://www.bbc.co.uk/news/world-africa-17015873).

Bernstein, Mary. 1997. "Celebration or Suppression: The Strategic Uses of Identity by the Gay and Lesbian Movements." *American Journal of Sociology* 103: 531–65.

Best, Joel. 2011. *The Stupidity Epidemic: Worrying about Schools, Students, and America's Future*. New York: Routledge.

———— 2013. *Social Problems*. New York: W.W. Norton & Co.

Best, Joel and Gerald T. Horiuchi. 1985. "The Razor Blade in the Apple: The Social Construction of Urban Legends." *Social Problems* 32: 488–99.

Billeaud, Jacques. 2013. "Dozens Protest Transfer of James Wilkerson, Air Force Officer Cleared of Sexual Assault Charges." *Huffington Post*, April 26. Retrieved July 31, 2013. (http://www. huffingtonpost.com/2013/04/26/james-wilkerson-sexual-assault_n_3162448.html).

Bivens, Josh. 2012. "Inequality, Exhibit A: Walmart and the Wealth of American Families." *Working Economics*, July 19 (http://www.epi.org/blog/inequality-exhibit-wal-mart-wealth-american).

Black, Michele C., Kathleen C. Basile, Matthew J. Breiding, Sharon G. Smith, Mikel L. Walters, Melissa T. Merrick, Jieru Chen, and Mark R. Stevens. 2011. *The National Intimate Partner and*

Sexual Violence Survey: 2010 Summary Report. Atlanta, GA: National Center for Injury Prevention and Control.

Blair-Smith, Eliot and Phil Kuntz. 2013. "Average CEO Pay Rations." *Bloomberg News*, April 30. Retrieved July 4, 2013 (http://go.bloomberg.com/multimedia/ceo-pay-ratio).

Blau, Judith and Alberto Moncado. 2009. *Human Rights: A Primer*. Boulder, CO: Paradigm Publishers.

BLS. 2013. "How the Government Measures Unemployment." Bureau of Labor Statistics. Retrieved July 4, 2013 (http://www.bls.gov/cps/cps_htgm.htm).

Bonds, Eric and Liam Downey. 2012. "'Green' Technologies and Unequal Ecological Exchange: The Environmental and Social Consequences of Ecological Modernization in the World System." *Journal of World-Systems Research* 18: 167–86.

Bonilla-Silva, Eduardo. 2009. *Racism without Racists: Color-Blind Racism and the Persistence of Racial Inequality in America*. Lanham, MD: Rowman & Littlefield.

Boyd, Cynthia. 2013. "Innovative Program Offers Low-Income Families More Fresh Fruit and Vegetables." *Minnesota Post*, June 25. Retrieved July 5, 2013 (http://www.minnpost.com/community-sketch-book/2013/06/innovative-program-offers-low-income-families-more-fresh-fruit-and-vege).

Brown, Robbie. 2012. "21 Chump Street." *This American Life*. Retrieved July 22, 2013 (http://www.thisamericanlife.org/radio-archives/episode/457/what-i-did-for-love?act=2).

Buffett, Warren E. 2011. "Stop Coddling the Super-Rich." *New York Times*, August 14. Retrieved July 5, 2013 (http://www.nytimes.com/2011/08/15/opinion/stop-coddling-the-super-rich.html).

Burns, Stewart. 1990. *Social Movements of the 1960s: Searching for Democracy*. New York: Twayne Publishing

Butler, Paul. 2009. *Let's get Free: A Hip-Hop Theory of Justice*. New York: The New Press.

Carson, E. Ann and William J. Sabol. 2012. "Prisoners in 2011." NCJ 239808. Washington, D.C.: Bureau of Justice Statistics.

CAWP. 2013. "Facts on Women in State Legislatures." *Center for American Women in Politics*. Retrieved July 29, 2013 (http://www.cawp.rutgers.edu/fast_facts/levels_of_office/state_legislature.php).

CBS News. 2011. "Anti Wall Street Protests from Coast to Coast." *CBS News*, Ocober 11. Retrieved July 19, 2013 (http://www.cbsnews.com/2300-201_162-10009714.html).

CIA. 2013a. "Country Comparison: Life Expectancy at Birth." *World Factbook*. Retrieved July 4, 2013 (https://www.cia.gov/library/publications/the-world-factbook/rankorder/2102rank.html).

———— 2013b. "Country Comparison: Infant Mortality Rate." *World Factbook*. Retrieved July 4, 2013 (https://www.cia.gov/library//publications/the-world-factbook/rankorder/2091rank.html).

———— 2013c. "Country Comparison: Distribution of Family Income." *World Factbook*. Retrieved July 4, 2013 (https://www.cia.gov/library/publications/the-world-factbook/rankorder/2172rank.html).

Conley, Dalton. 1999. *Being Black, Living in the Red: Race, Wealth, and Social Policy in America*. Berkeley: University of California Press.

Cook and Cook. 2012. "Current and Historical Federal Estate Tax Structure, Exemptions and Rates." Cooklaw Blog, December 17. Retrieved July 5, 2013 (http://cooklaw.co/blog/current-historical-federal-estate-tax-structure-exemptions-rates).

CRP. 2012. "Reelection Rates Over the Years." *Center for Responsive Politics*. Retrieved January 29, 2014 (https://www.opensecrets.org/bigpicture/reelect.php?cycle=2012).

———— 2013a. "Price of Admission." *Center for Responsive Politics*. Retrieved July 7, 2013 (http://www.opensecrets.org/bigpicture/stats.php).

———— 2013b. "2012 Presidential Race." *Center for Responsive Politics*. Retrieved July 7, 2013 (http://www.opensecrets.org/pres12/index.php).

———— 2013c. "Top Overall Contributors." *Center for Responsive Politics*. Retrieved July 6, 2013 (http://www.opensecrets.org/overview/topindivs_overall.php).

———— 2013d. "Donor Demographics." *Center for Responsive Politics*. Retrieved July 7, 2013 (http://www.opensecrets.org/overview/donordemographics.php).

———— 2013e. "Incumbent Advantage." *Center for Responsive Politics*. Retrieved July 7, 2013 (http://www.opensecrets.org/overview/incumbs.php).

Dalbert, Paula. 2013. "Brazil Protesters Keep up the Pressure." *al Jazeera*, August 1. Retrieved September 3, 2013 (http://www.aljazeera.com/indepth/features/2013/07/2013730121211201331.html).

DeNavas-Walt, Carmen, Bernadette D. Proctor, and Jessica C. Smith. 2012. *Income, Poverty and Health Insurance in the United States: 2011*. Washington, D.C.: U.S. Census Bureau.

Domhoff, G. William. 2009. *Who Rules America: Challenges to Corporate and Class Dominance*. New York: McGraw Hill Education.

Douglas, Frederick. 1857. *West Indian Emancipation*. Speech delivered at Canandaigua, New York, August 3. Retrieved September 3, 2013 (http://www.lib.rochester.edu/index.cfm?PAGE=4398).

Downey, Liam, Eric Bonds, and Catherine Clark. 2010. "Natural Resource Extraction, Armed Violence, and Environmental Degradation." *Organization and Environment* 23: 417–45.

Duhigg, Charles and David Barboza. 2012. "In China, Human Costs are Built into an iPad." *New York Times*, January 25. Retrieved August 26, 2013 (http://www.nytimes.com/2012/01/26/business/ieconomy-apples-ipad-and-the-human-costs-for-workers-in-china.html?pagewanted=all).

Dyson, Michael E. 2001. *I May Not Get There with You: The True Martin Luther King, Jr.* New York: The Free Press.

Elliot, Kimberly. 2012. "Is My Fair Trade Coffee Really Fair? Trends and Challenges in Fair Trade Certification." *Center for Global Development*, December 12 Policy Paper. Retrieved August 26, 2013 (http://www.cgdev.org/publication/my-fair-trade-coffee-really-fair-trends-and-challenges-fair-trade-certification).

Essa, Azad. 2013. "The Meaning of Marikana." *al Jazeera*, August 16. Retrieved August 26, 2013 (http://www.nytimes.com/2012/08/31/world/africa/south-africa-to-charge-marikana-miners-in-deadly-unrest.html?_r=0).

Fair Trade USA. 2013. "2012 Almanac." *Impact Report from Fair Trade USA*. Retrieved August 26, 2013 (http://fairtradeusa.org/sites/default/files/2012_Fair-Trade-USA_Almanac.pdf).

Featherstone, Liza. 2002. *Students Against Sweatshops: The Making of a Movement*. London: Verso.

Fisher, Gordon M. 1997. "The Development of the Orshansky Poverty Thresholds and Their Subsequent History as the Official U.S. Poverty Measure." U.S. Census Bureau. Retrieved July 2, 2013 (http://www.census.gov/hhes/povmeas/publications/orshansky.html).

Forbes. 2012. "The Forbes 400: The Richest People in America." *Forbes*, September 19. Retrieved July 4, 2013 (http://www.forbes.com/forbes-400).

Fox, Emily J. 2013. "Wal-Mart's Low Wages Cost Taxpayers." *CNN Money*, June 5. Retrieved July 4, 2013 (http://money.cnn.com/2013/06/04/news/companies/walmart-medicaid/index.html).

Fox News. 2012. "Internet Addiction Causes Brain Changes Similar to Alcohol and Drugs, Study Finds." *Fox News*, January 12. Retrieved January 29, 2014 (http://www.foxnews.com/health/2012/01/12/internet-addiction-causes-brain-changes-similar-to-alcohol-and-drugs-study).

Froomkin, Dan. 2013. "It Can't Happen Here: Why Is There So Little Coverage of Americans Who Are Struggling With Poverty?" *Nieman Reports*, Winter Issue. Retrieved July 4, 2013 (http://www.nieman.harvard.edu/reports/article/102832/It-Cant-Happen-Here.aspx).

Galeano, Eduardo. 1973. *The Open Veins of Latin America: Five Centuries of the Pillage of a Continent*. New York: Monthly Review Press.

Garside, Juliette. 2012. "Apple's Factories in China are Breaking Employment Laws, Audit Finds." *Guardian*, March 29. Retrieved August 26, 2013 (http://www.theguardian.com/technology/2012/mar/30/apple-factories-china-foxconn-audit).

Gidycz, Christine A., Lindsay M. Orchowski, and Alan D. Berkowitz. 2011. "Preventing Sexual Aggression Among College Men: An Evaluation of a Social Norms and Bystander Intervention Program." *Violence Against Women* 17: 720–42.

Gilson, Dave. 2012. "How Much have the Kochs Spent on the Election?" *Mother Jones*, November 5. Retrieved July 19, 2013 (http://www.motherjones.com/politics/2012/11/charts-map-koch-brothers-2012-spending).

Goldman, Michael. 2006. *Imperial Nature: The World Bank and Struggles for Social Justice in the Age of Globalization*. New Haven, CT: Yale University Press.

Goodman, Amy and Denis Moynihan. 2013. "Addressing the Epidemic of Military Sexual Assault." *Democracy Now*, May 9. Retrieved July 31, 2013 (http://www.democracynow.org/blog/2013/5/9/addressing_the_epidemic_of_military_sexual_assault).

Guinness Records. 2014. "Most Translated Document: Universal Declaration of Human Rights." Retrieved January 29, 2014 (http://www.guinnessworldrecords.com/records-1000/most-translated-document).

Heiner, Robert. 2012. *Social Problems: An Introduction to Critical Constructionism*. New York: Oxford University Press.

Horowitz, Jason. 2011. "Grover Norquist, the Anti-Tax Enforcer Behind the Scenes in the Debt Debate." *Washington Post*, July 12. Retrieved July 4, 2013 (http://articles.washingtonpost.com/2011-07-12/lifestyle/35236400_1_grover-norquist-debt-talks-americans-for-tax-reform).

ICG. 2012. "Conflict Minerals in DRC." *International Crisis Group*, January 12. Retrieved August 26, 2013 (http://www.crisisgroup.org/en/publication-type/key-issues/country/conflict-minerals-in-drc.aspx).

Jensen, Robert. 1998. "White Privilege Shapes the U.S." *Baltimore Sun*, July 19. Retrieved January 29, 2014 (http://uts.cc.utexas.edu/~rjensen/freelance/whiteprivilege.htm).

Jones, Van. 2008. *The Green Collar Economy: How One Solution Can Fix Our Two Biggest Problems*. New York: HarperCollins.

King, Martin Luther. 1963. *Letter from a Birmingham Jail*. Retrieved September 3, 2013 (http://www.nytimes.com/2013/03/28/us/maine-lawyer-credited-in-fight-for-gay-marriage.html?pagewanted=all).

——— 1965. *Our God Is Marching On*. Speech delivered in Montgomery, AL on March 25. Retrieved September 3, 2013 (http://mlk-kpp01.stanford.edu/index.php/kingpapers/article/our_god_is_marching_on).

———— 1967. *Beyond Vietnam*. Speech delivered at New York City's Riverside Church on April 4. Retrieved September 3, 2013 (http://www.democracynow.org/2013/1/21/dr_martin_luther_king_in_1967).

Kingkade, Tyler. 2013. "USC Student: Police Said I Wasn't Raped Because He Didn't Orgasm." *Huffington Post*, July 22. Retrieved July 31, 2013 (http://www.huffingtonpost.com/2013/07/22/usc-rape-investigation_n_3607954.html).

Krebs, Christopher P., Christine H. Lindquist, Tara D. Warner, Bonnie S. Fisher, and Sandra L. Martin. 2009. "College Women's Experiences with Physically Forced, Alcohol or Other Drug-Enabled, and Drug-Facilitated Sexual Assault Before and Since Entering College." *Journal of American College Health* 56: 639–49.

Lee, Chris. 2011. "The Sex Addiction Epidemic." *Newsweek*, November 25. Retrieved February 1, 2013 (www.thedailybeast.com/newsweek/2011/11/27/the-sex-addiction-epidemic.html).

Lee, Trymaine. 2012. "Marissa Alexander, Florida Mom, Faces Mandatory 20 Years In Prison After Failed Stand-Your-Ground Defense." *Huffington Post*, May 2. Retrieved July 22 (http://www.huffingtonpost.com/2012/05/02/marissa-alexander-florida-stand-your-ground_n_1472647.html).

Lessig, Lawrence. 2011. *Republic Lost: How Money Corrupts Congress and a Plan to Stop It*. New York: Twelve.

Lester, T. William and Ken Jacobs. 2010. *Creating Good Jobs in Our Communities: How Higher Wage Standards Affect Economic Development and Employment*. Washington, D.C.: Center for American Progress. Retrieved July 5, 2013 (http://www.americanprogressaction.org/issues/labor/report/2010/11/30/8599/creating-good-jobs-in-our-communities).

Lowry, Anne. 2013. "Wealth Gap Among Races Has Widened Since Recession." *New York Times*, April 28. Retrieved July 23, 2013 (http://www.nytimes.com/2013/04/29/business/racial-wealth-gap-widened-during-recession.html?pagewanted=all).

McAdam, Doug. 1983. "Tactical Innovation and the Pace of Insurgency." *American Sociological Review* 48: 735–54.

McCarthy, Diane. 2011. "Ghana Farmers Lose Out in Gold Mining Boom." *CNN*, December 12. Retrieved August 26, 2013 (http://www.cnn.com/2011/12/12/world/africa/ghana-gold-owusu-koranteng).

Macartney, Suzanne, Alemayehu Bishaw, and Kayla Fontenot. 2013. "Poverty Rates for Selected Detailed Race and Hispanic Groups by State and Place: 2007–2011." U.S. Department of Commerce. *American Community Survey Briefs, ACSBR/11-17*. Washington D.C.: U.S. Census Bureau.

Mason, Paul. 2013. *Why It's Still Kicking Off Everywhere*. London: Verso.

Mayer, Jane. 2010. "Covert Operations: The Billionaire Brothers Who Are Waging a War Against Obama." *New Yorker*, August 30. Retrieved July 19, 2013 (http://www.newyorker.com/reporting/2010/08/30/100830fa_fact_mayer?currentPage=all).

Merton, Robert K. 1995. "The Thomas Theorem and The Matthew Effect." *Social Forces*, 74: 379–424.

Miller, John. 2004. "Tax Wealth: Great Political Economists and Andrew Carnegie Agree." Pp. 111–16 in *Wealth Inequality Reader*, ed. Chuck Collins and Amy Gluckman. Cambridge, MA: Dollars and Sense.

Mishel, Lawerence. 2012. "Confirming the Further Upward Redistribution of Wealth." *Working Economics*, July 20. Retrieved July 4, 2013 (http://www.epi.org/blog/confirming-redistribution-wealth-upward).

Mohamed, A. Rafik and Erik D. Fritsvold. 2011. *Dorm Room Dealers: Drugs and the Privileges of Race and Class.* Boulder, CO: Lynne Rienner.

Morsink, Johannes. 1999. *The Universal Declaration of Human Rights.* Philadelphia: University of Pennsylvania Press.

Mungin, Lateef. 2013. "College Women Told to Urinate or Vomit to Deter a Rapist." *CNN*, February 20. Retrieved July 29, 2013 (http://www.cnn.com/2013/02/20/justice/colorado-rape-prevention-guidelines).

Nichols, John. 2013. "America's Most Dynamic (Yet Under-Covered) Movement: Overturning 'Citizens United.'" *The Nation*, July 7. Retrieved July 8, 2013 (http://www.commondreams.org/view/2013/07/07-2).

NLCHP. 2011. *Criminalization Crisis: The Criminalization of Homelessness in U.S. Cities.* Washington, D.C.: National Law Center on Homelessness and Poverty. Retrieved July 4, 2013 (http://www.nlchp.org/content/pubs/11.14.11%20Criminalization%20Report%20&%20Advocacy%20Manual,%20FINAL1.pdf).

NRC (National Research Council). (2008). *Minerals, Critical Minerals, and the U.S. Economy.* Washington, D.C.: National Academies Press.

NYCLU. 2013. "Stop and Frisk 2012." *New York Civil Liberties Union.* Retrieved July 23, 2013 (http://www.nyclu.org/files/publications/2012_Report_NYCLU_0.pdf).

Obama, Barack. 2013. "Remarks by the President in the State of the Union Speech." White House Release, February 12. Retrieved July 5, 2013 (http://www.whitehouse.gov/the-press-office/2013/02/12/remarks-president-state-union-address).

OPEC. 2012. "Nigeria Facts and Figures." *OPEC Annual Statistical Bulletin 2012.* Retrieved August 26, 2013 (http://www.opec.org/opec_web/en/about_us/167.htm).

Oskin, Becky. 2013. "Radioactive Mountain Is Key in US Rare-Earth Woes." *LiveScience*, June 11. Retrieved August 26, 2013 (http://www.livescience.com/37356-heavy-rare-earth-mining-america.html).

Pear, Robert. 2013. "Median Income Rises, but Is Still 6% Below Level at Start of Recession in '07." *New York Times*, August 31. Retrieved September 3, 2013 (http://www.nytimes.com/2013/08/22/us/politics/us-median-income-rises-but-is-still-6-below-its-2007-peak.html).

Pinker, Steven. 2012. *The Better Angels of Our Nature: Why Violence Has Declined.* New York: Penguin.

Poggiolo, Sylva. 2012. "German Lawmakers Move To Quell Uproar Over Circumcision." *National Public Radio*, October 19. Retrieved July 4, 2013 (http://www.npr.org/blogs/health/2012/10/19/163268294/german-lawmakers-move-to-quell-uproar-over-circumcision).

Polgreen, Lydia. 2012. "In Police Shooting of Miners, South Africa Charges Miners." *New York Times*, August 12. Retrieved August 26, 2013 (http://www.nytimes.com/2012/08/31/world/africa/south-africa-to-charge-marikana-miners-in-deadly-unrest.html?_r=0).

Provine, Doris M. 2011. "Race and Inequality in the War on Drugs." *Annual Review of Law and Social Science* 7: 41–60.

QP. 2013. "Argentina." *The Quota Project: Global Database of Quotas for Women.* Retrieved July 29, 2013 (http://www.quotaproject.org/uid/countryview.cfm?ul=en&country=12).

Rich, Motoko. 2012. "How Head Start Can Make a Difference." *New York Times*, March 2. Retrieve July 5, 2013 (http://economix.blogs.nytimes.com/2012/03/02/how-head-start-can-make-a-difference).

Robinson, William I. and Mario Barrera. 2012. "Global Capitalism and Twenty-First Century Fascism: A U.S. Case Study." *Race and Class* 53: 4–29.

Saenz, Arlette. 2013. "Military Sexual Assault Victims Testify Before Congress." *ABC News*, March 13. Retrieved July 31 (http://abcnews.go.com/blogs/politics/2013/03/military-sexual-assault-victims-testify-before-congress).

SAMHS. 2012. *Results from the 2011 National Survey on Drug Use and Health: Summary of National Findings*, NSDUH Series H-44, HHS Publication no. (SMA) 12-4713. Rockville, MD: Substance Abuse and Mental Health Services Administration.

Sardi, Lauren. 2011. "The Male Neonatal Circumcision Debate: Social Movements, Sexual Citizenship, and Human Rights." *Societies Without Borders: Human Rights and the Social Sciences* 6(3): 304–29.

Schwindt-Bayer, Leslie A. 2009. "Making Quotas Work: The Effect of Gender Quotas on the Election of Women." *Legislative Studies Quarterly* 34: 5–28.

Seidman, Gay. 2009. *Beyond the Boycott: Labor Rights, Human Rights, and Transnational Activism*. New York: Sage.

Sen, Amartya. 1999. *Development as Freedom*. New York: Random House.

Shapiro, Thomas M. and Melvin L. Oliver. 1997. *Black Wealth/White Wealth: A New Perspective*. New York: Routledge.

Short, Kathleen. 2013. "The Research Supplemental Poverty Measure: 2012." *Current Population Report, U.S. Census Bureau*. Retrieved December 16 (http://www.census.gov/prod/2013pubs/p60-247.pdf).

Sjoberg, Gideon, Elizabeth A. Gill and Norma Williams. 2001. "A Sociology of Human Rights." *Social Problems* 48(1): 11–47.

SMAHS. 2012. *Results from the 2011 National Survey on Drug Use and Health: Summary of National Findings*, HHS Publication no. (SMA) 12-4713. Rockville, MD: Substance Abuse and Mental Health Services Administration.

Smith, Jackie and Dawn Wiest. 2012. *Social Movements in the World-System: The Politics of Crisis and Transformation*. New York: Russell Sage Foundation.

Smooth, Jay. 2011. "How I Learned to Stop Worrying and Love to Talk About Race." TEDxHampshire Talk, November 15. Retrieved July 23, 2013 (http://www.youtube.com/watch?v=MbdxeFcQtaU).

Spector, Malcolm and John I. Kitsuse. 1977. *Constructing Social Problems*. Menlo Park, CA: Cummings Publishing Co.

Stolberg, Sheryl G. 2013. "In Fight for Gay Marriage, 'She's our Thurgood Marshall.'" *New York Times*, March 27. Retrieved September 3, 2013 (http://www.nytimes.com/2013/03/28/us/maine-lawyer-credited-in-fight-for-gay-marriage.html?pagewanted=all).

Taylor, Adam. 2012. "Here's What College Education Costs Students Around The World." *Business Insider*, June 12. Retrieved July 5, 2013 (http://www.businessinsider.com/tuition-costs-by-country-college-higher-education-2012-6).

Taylor, Nick. 2008. *American-Made: The Enduring Legacy of the WPA*. New York: Bantam Books.

Teigen, Mari. 2012. "Firms, Boards and Gender Quotas: Comparative Perspectives." *Comparative Social Research* 29: 115–46.

Terkel, Amanda and Ryan Grim. 2012. "Koch Brothers, Allies Pledge $100 Million at Private Meeting to Beat Obama." *Huffington Post*, February 6. Retrieved July 19, 2013 (http://www.huffingtonpost.com/2012/02/03/koch-brothers-100-million-obama_n_1250828.html).

Thomas, Landon. 2006. "A $31 Billion Gift Between Friends." *New York Times*, June 27. Retrieved July 5, 2013 (http://www.nytimes.com/2006/06/27/business/27friends.html?_r=0).

Tilly, Charles. 1990. *Coercion, Capital, and European States, AD 990–1990*. Cambridge: Basil Blackwell.

Turner, Bryan S. 2006. *Vulnerability and Human Rights*. Philadelphia: Pennsylvania University Press.

Ulrich, Monika. 2011. "Using Drunk Driving Deaths to Understand Sexual Assault." *TRAILS: Teaching Resources and Innovations Library for Sociology*. Washington DC: American Sociological Association.

UN. 2013. "Growth in United Nations Membership, 1945–Present." United Nations website. Retrieved July 4, 2013 (http://www.un.org/en/members/growth.shtml).

United for a Fair Economy. 2012. *Born on Third Base: What the Forbes 400 Really Says About Economic Equality and Opportunity in America*. Washington D.C.: United for a Fair Economy. Retrieved July 4, 2013 (http://faireconomy.org/sites/default/files/BornOnThirdBase2012.pdf).

Wagner, Steve. 2012. "Incarceration Is Not an Equal Opportunity Punishment." *Prison Policy Institute*, August 28. Retrieved July 23, 2013 (http://www.prisonpolicy.org/articles/notequal.html).

Wallerstein, Immanuel. 2004. *World-Systems Analysis: An Introduction*. London: Duke University Press.

——— 2011. *Centrist Liberalism Triumphant, 1789–1914*. Berkeley: University of California Press.

Wilkie, Christina. 2013. "Conflict Minerals Law Is Heavy Burden On Business, House Republicans Argue." *Huffington Post*, May 22. Retrieved August 26, 2013 (http://www.huffingtonpost.com/2013/05/22/conflict-minerals-law_n_3322395.html).

Wing, Nick. 2013. "Moral Monday Protest Draws Crowd Against North Carolina Voter ID, Leads to 73 More Arrests." *Huffington Post*, July 23. Retrieved July 23, 2013 (http://www.huffingtonpost.com/2013/07/23/moral-monday-protest_n_3639208.html?utm_hp_ref=politics).

Wolitzky-Taylor, Kate B., Heidi S. Resnick, Amanda B. Amstadter, Jenna L. McCauley, Kenneth J. Ruggiero, and Dean G. Kilpatrick. 2011. "Reporting of Rape in a National Sample of Women." *Journal of American College Health* 59: 582–87.

Glossary/Index

Note: Page numbers followed by 'f' refer to figures and followed by 't' refer to tables.

A

absolute measure of poverty: defined as the inability to access the basic conditions that make human life possible 19

activism: participation in a social movement or other efforts to promote social change outside elections and political campaigns 39, 57–58, 62–65

Alexander, Marissa 32, 35, 38, 39, 40

American Civil Liberties Union: the ACLU has been one of the most effective organizations that has, since 1920, defended and promoted civil and political rights in America. Its website is: www.aclu.org 36

Americans for Tax Reform 19

Amnesty International: one of the largest and most prominent international human rights organizations. Founded in 1961, it has primarily focused on protecting civil and political rights from government abuse. Its website is: http://www.amnesty.org 6

Anti Drug Abuse Act 1986 35

Arab Spring 1, 66, 67

Argentina 49

austerity: cuts or limitations on the amount of public spending 19, 67

automation of work: the introduction of robotics or other technologies to reduce labor costs, resulting in fewer jobs for the same levels of production 14, 66

B

Best, Joel 2, 3, 4

Birmingham, Alabama 64

bodily integrity, violation of right to 42–43

Bolivia 1, 53, 54–55

Bouazizi, Mohamed 1

Brazil 52, 67

Brown vs. Board of Education 64

Buffett, Warren 21
Butler, Paul 39–40

C
careers of social problems: the idea, advocated by Spector and Kitsuse (1977) that social problems can be studied by uncovering their origin, their amplification in the news media, and their eventual demise 4
Carnegie, Andrew 21
cell phones 51–53
China 51, 52
circumcision 7
Citizens United vs. FEC 24–25, 29
civil disobedience: the intentional violation of unjust laws in order to promote social change 39
Civil Rights Act 1964 64
Civil Rights Movement: the powerful American social movement of the 1950s and 1960s that overturned the legal and political exclusion of African Americans common in the Jim Crow era, but had less success in challenging poverty and the economic exclusion of people of color 21, 33, 37, 60, 63–64
civil society: those elements of public life that take place outside of the institutions of government and business. Important civil society institutions include professional and civic organizations along with nonprofit advocacy groups. 6
claims-making: the process of calling attention to some aspect of the world and labeling it a problem 2–3, 4
clothing industry 57–58
cocaine and crack cocaine 35–36
colonialism: an inequitable relationship between peoples, maintained through the use or threat of military violence, in which one territory or society is administered for the benefit of another 7, 33, 53, 55–56, 66
colorblind racism: refers to statements that approve of the abolition of intentional forms of racism but also overlook the ways that racism has been structured into our economy and society 38
consciousness-raising groups: a tactic used in the **Second Wave** of the Women's Movement to help women understand the commonality of their experiences and the shared nature of their oppression 63
constitutional amendments, proposed 29, 30, 46
Convention on the Elimination of All Forms of Discrimination against Women (CEDAW) 46
critical minerals: specific materials that are essential to technology and infrastructure used in the U.S. economy, but that mostly come from outside the United States 54, 54t

cultural strategy of social change: efforts to secure human rights by working to change people's attitudes and understandings of the world 63

D

deindustrialization: the process, beginning in the late 1970s, by which U.S. corporations shifted manufacturing overseas 54

democracy vouchers 29

democratic participation, right to 24
    proposed constitutional amendment 29, 30
    running for political office 25–26, 26t, 28
    striking a balance 29–30
    undermining of 26–28

Democratic Republic of Congo (DRC) 52, 58

dignity, right to 11–14

Douglas, Frederick 65

drugs decriminalization 39–40

drugs war 33–38

E

economy 15, 18, 66
    racism in 36, 37

Eighteenth Amendment 29

election campaign 2012 24, 25, 26, 26t

electronic manufacturers 58

Equal Rights Amendment Act (ERA) 46

estate tax 20, 22

F

Fair Trade: a third-party certification that ensures that a product was made under conditions that promoted and protected workers' wellbeing 56–57

Fair Trade USA 57

feminist: a person who works to protect and advance human rights for women 49

Fifteenth Amendment 33

First Amendment 24

Food Stamp Act 1964 14

Foxconn 52

free speech, right to 24–25
    U.S.Supreme Court interpretations of 24, 28, 29

funding, political 24, 25–27, 26t, 27, 28
    proposed constitutional amendment on 29, 30

future of human rights 67–68

G

Galeano, Eduardo 53

Gay and Lesbian Movement 62, 63

Gini index 15, 16t

global economic crisis 65–66

global economy, human rights in 53–56

efforts to promote 56–58

global race to the bottom: the downward pressure on wages, taxes, and environmental regulations due to the mobility of multinational corporations 55, 56

Global South: a term that does not refer exclusively to nations in the Earth's southern hemisphere, but to nations that were formally colonized by European powers. This term is also used to refer to what used to be called the "Third World." 53–54, 56

globalization: while the world economy is very old, this concept refers to the recent intensification of global economic production that began in the 1970s 14, 53–54

Great Depression 6, 14–15

Greece 13, 67

H

harm reduction approach: an alternative to the "war on drugs," based on the idea that decriminalization can lead to more effective ways to limit the harm caused by drug addictions 39–40

Havrilla, Rebekah 43

Hawaii 62

Head Start: a federal program, founded in 1965, to promote early childhood education for families that would otherwise not be able to afford preschool 14

healthcare, access to 13

higher education, access to 13–14

human rights

approach to social problems 4–8

defining 1–2

I

Iceland 49

ideology: a worldview that has political implications and effects. According to some Marxist and other critical sociologists, the ability to shape ideology is an important form of power that can be used to maintain or extend inequality. 18

income

after global economic crisis 66

comparing CEO and average employee compensation 16, 17t

distribution 15–16, 16f, 16t

of women 45

indignity: social pain caused when one is deprived of conditions that constitute full personhood in a particular society 5

indium 54, 54t

infant mortality 13

inherited wealth 18, 20–21, 22

insecurity: concern about one's ability to regularly secure the material conditions—food, shelter, and clean water—that make life possible 5

institutional corruption: refers to the ways that campaign contributions influence a politician's behavior 27–28

institutional racism: this term was coined by Stokely Carmichael in the late 1960s, based on his and other black leaders' recognition that ending legal forms of discrimination in the United States would not in itself bring about racial equality. Rather, because racism was so embedded in U.S. economic, political, and educational institutions over the past several hundred years, it continues to create racist outcomes today. 36

International Monetary Fund: a multilateral organization created in 1944 to promote global financial stability, frequently requiring nations to enact policies of austerity in order to receive loans 56

J

Jim Crow segregation: legal policies that separate and exclude people based on perceptions of race 33, 36

Jones, Van 15

K

King, Martin Luther 60, 65

Koch, David and Charles 24

L

labor conditions 52

Laboy, Justin 33–34

law in a patriarchal society 45–46

law, right to be treated equally before 32–40
    comparison of two cases in Florida 32
    and promotion of racial justice 38–40
    UN Declaration on Human Rights and 32–33
    and "War on Drugs" 33–38

legal strategy of social change: efforts to secure human rights by filing lawsuits in order to abolish discriminatory laws 62

Lessig, Lawrence 27, 29

"Letter from a Birmingham Jail" 65

life-expectancy 13

living wage: a wage that is sufficient to provide for a life with dignity, commensurate with the cost of living in different locations 21–22

M

mandatory minimum: laws that require a predetermined time behind bars for convictions of particular crimes, regardless of extenuating circumstances 39

Martin, Trayvon 32, 39

Marx, Karl 20, 53

Mason, Paul 66–67

media

    coverage on poverty 18

    objectification of women 47

    reporting on social problems 4

moral relativism: the position that, because values differ depending upon cultural and historical context, there is no definitive answer to questions about what is good and just 5

N

NAACP: the National Association for the Advancement of Colored People, founded in 1909, on the anniversary of Abraham Lincoln's birthday. Founded only 24 years after the abolition of slavery, it is the oldest civil rights organization in the United States. It has challenged the systematic violence and denial of rights to black Americans, and two of its founders, W.E.B. Du Bois and Ida B. Wells-Barnett, are also major figures in U.S. sociology. Its website is: http://www.naacp.org 39, 63–64

Nazi genocide 6

The New Jim Crow 35

New York "stop and frisk" policy 37, 39

Nigeria 55

nonprofit organizations: refers to a broad range of groups, from charities to environmental organizations to sports clubs, that are funded primarily through donations 61

nonviolence: the strategic use of civil disobedience, as famously articulated and practiced by such leaders as Mahatma Gandhi and Martin Luther King Jr., exercised to create a constructive tension that compels power-holders to enter into negotiations with challengers 64

Norway 49

O

Obama, Barack 14, 24, 25, 26

objectification: the portrayal of human beings as objects that exist for others' gratification 47

Occupy Movement 1, 10, 66
The Open Veins of Latin America 53

P
palladium 51–52, 54t
patriarchal: a society that privileges men and in which men hold a disproportionate share of power, wealth, status, and leadership positions 45–47
pay *see* income
personal corruption: refers to the granting of personal gifts or rewards to influence a politician's behavior 27
personal racism: individual behaviors that advantage and disadvantage others based upon perceptions of race 36
pink-collar jobs: occupational categories that have been associated with "women's work," and which are typically less well paid compared to jobs with comparable skill and educational requirements in more male-dominated fields 45
Pinker, Steven 65
platinum 51, 54t
pluralism: the belief that no one group holds disproportionate influence in a political system, but rather that power is shared between shifting coalitions of different political groups 24–25, 26
policing policies 34–35, 36, 37, 39
political action committees (PACS): organizations that exist to raise and spend money to elect or defeat political candidates. They offer wealthy persons a way to spend money on elections beyond the federal caps on individual donations. 25
political action to promote human rights 62–65
politics
    funding 24, 25–27, 26t, 27, 28, 29, 30
    and law 45–46
    running for office 25–26, 26t, 28
    striking a balance between political rights 29–30
    undermining of democratic rights in 26–28
    wealth and power in 18, 20, 28
    women in 46, 49
Potosí, Bolivia 53, 54–55
poverty 11–13, 18–19
  in Nigeria 55
  by race 36, 37f
power: a concept referring both to a group's collective ability to achieve shared goals and a relationship of domination between different groups 8
    wealth and political 18, 20, 28
    women in positions of 49

sexism: social processes that advantage some and disadvantage others based upon their gender or sex 45–47

sexual assault: unwanted sexual touching, including rape 41
institutional interventions to prevent 47–48
in social context 43–47

silver mining 53, 54–55

SNAP: the Supplemental Nutrition Assistance Program, formerly known as the Food Stamp Program in its pilot form (1939–1943), was created in 1965 as part of President Lyndon Johnson's "War on Poverty." The aim of both programs has been to eliminate hunger and malnutrition in the United States. 14

social constructionism: the sociological perspective that humans do not act on the world itself, but based on interpretations of that world 2–4, 5

social movement: a group of individuals and organizations working to promote social change outside political campaigns and elections *see also* **Civil Rights Movement** 33, 39, 58, 62–63, 64, 66–67
Arab Spring 1, 66, 67
Occupy Movement 1, 10, 66
women's organizations 63
World Social Forum 58

social problems: a concept that is defined differently by different sociological perspectives. The perspective used in this book is that a social problem occurs when a group's human rights are violated or left unfilled. 2
human rights approach 4–8
social construction of 2–4

social structure: the durable organization of society, typically marked by inequalities in power and resources between groups, that is reproduced over time 18

social welfare group (501(c)4): an organization that, in the new political landscape created by the Supreme Court's 2010 decision in *Citizens United vs. the FEC*, can spend unlimited amounts of money to influence elections and is not required to publicly disclose the names of its contributors 25

South Africa 51

Spain 49, 66

"stop and frisk" policy 37, 39

"stupidity epidemics" 2, 3

Supplemental Nutrition Assistance Program *see* SNAP

Supplemental Poverty Measure 12

T
tantalum 52

U

Ulrich, Monica 48

underdevelopment: the result of colonization or contemporary inequitable relationships between nations that can result in the loss of natural resource wealth, environmental degradation, and increased poverty 54–55

unemployment 6, 13, 14, 66

unequal exchange: inequitable relationships of trade between nations in the Global
South and Global North 55–56

Universal Declaration of Human Rights: a statement adopted by the United Nations
in 1948 that sought to "establish a common standard of achievement for all peoples and all nations." The document has inspired both grassroots and international
political movements, while also providing a foundation for several international
treaties, such as the International Covenant on Economic, Social and Cultural
Rights, the International Covenant on Civil and Political Rights, and the United
Nations Convention Against Torture. 6–8, 32–33, 69–75

    measuring U.S. against goals of 12, 13, 14, 19, 64

universities

    clothing certification schemes 57–58

    drinking policies 44

    and feminist organizations 49

    interventions to prevent sexual assault 47–48

    sexual assault in 41, 43, 44

University of Colorado 41, 47

University of Southern California 41

U.S. Census Bureau: the U.S. agency created to gather and tabulate demographic
data about the U.S. population. The agency developed and institutionalized a
measure of poverty that has been consequential for both sociological practice and
U.S. political life. 12

U.S. military 43–44

U.S. Supreme Court 24, 28, 29, 63, 64

V

volunteerism: efforts to satisfy human needs and improve communities through
unpaid work 61–62

vote, right to 33, 34, 39, 45

W

Wal-Mart 18, 19

Walton, Sam 18

We Are The 99 Percent 10–11

wealth: total assets owned subtracted by debts, often a better indicator of economic inequality than income 15–18, 17f

inherited 18, 20–21, 22

and political power 18, 20, 28

and race 36

wellbeing

achieving for all 14–15

compromising of right to 11–14

striking a balance between property ownership and 20–22

white privilege: unearned rewards that people socially classified as "white" receive due to the historic legacy and continued operation of racism in America 35, 67

Wilkerson, James 44

women

objectification of 47

pay 45

in politics 46, 49

in power 49

in a sexist society 43–47

Women's Movement 46, 49, 63

women's rights 47–49

World Bank: a multilateral organization founded in 1944 that provides loans to finance development projects in the Global South. These loans, however, frequently benefit multinational corporations much more than local community members. The president of the World Bank has always been an American. 56

World Social Forum 58

Z

Zimmerman, George 32

THE SOCIAL ISSUES COLLECTION™

Finally, it's easy to
customize materials for your sociology course

Choose from a collection of 250 readings from Routledge and other publishers to create a perfect anthology that fits your course and students.

1 Go to the website at socialissuescollection.com **2** Choose from 250 readings in sociology **3** Create your complete custom anthology

Readings from The Social Issues Collection are pre-cleared and available at reduced permission rates, helping your students save money on course materials. Projects are ready in 2 weeks for direct e-commerce student purchases.

For over 25 undergraduate sociology courses including:

Criminology	Globalization	Social Inequalities
Cultural Sociology	Sociology of Work and Economy	Sociology of Media and Communication
Environmental Sociology	Marriage and Family	Sociology of Place
Gender	Race and Ethnicity	Sociology of Religion

Contact us to learn more about our services

3970 Sorrento Valley Blvd. Ste 500, San Diego, CA 92121 I info@universityreaders.com I 800-200-3908 x 501

University Readers is an imprint of Cognella, Inc. ©1997-2012